What People Are Saying About This Book

Engaged Couples

"This material was instrumental in teaching us to think spiritually during our dating relationship. The scriptures and practical exercises prepared us for all of the joys and challenges that come with marriage." —Joe Senter, Durham, NC

"We were really fortunate to have Randall's pre-marriage materials to build a foundation on. Without it, we would not have known some of the big topics that needed to be discussed and thought about beforehand. Because of it, we were well prepared, had developed great communication skills, and were able to relax and enjoy the first few years of our marriage!"
—Cory and Erin Kraftchick, Raleigh, NC

"*Preparing to Live As One* leads you through the process of recognizing that your mate has different needs than you do, and you need to make a conscious effort to meet them, daily. Also, I have noted 'accept as you want to be accepted,' which really gets to the heart of the 'how do I fix my mate' question. Timeless information: The tools that you learn (or are reminded of) are applicable in the first year of marriage as well as the 51st. A wise disciple would review and do the exercises periodically."
—Jim Krozser, Raleigh, NC

"A lot of couples talk about their first year of marriage being the hardest. That's especially true for those like me who were single and on their own for a long time before getting married. But our first year of marriage was fantastic (and just getting better!), and I attribute that to the counseling we received going through this material before the wedding day. We were able to discuss our expectations and ideas of what marriage would be, from how we would handle disagreements down to who would take out the trash. Going through each chapter helped me to understand my fiancé in a deeper way and provided the framework for discussing issues that we had never addressed as a dating couple. I was able to decide what kind of wife I wanted to be for him and make a commitment to what I would do (and would not allow myself to do) in order to make my marriage strong. We are eternally grateful for the opportunity to address these challenges before we tied the knot!"
—Melissa Alford, Raleigh, NC

Mentoring Couples

"Through many years of counseling marriages it is obvious to us that couples are oft ill-prepared for the challenges of living daily as 'one.' Starry-eyed infatuation can quickly turn to wild-eyed frustration when two people discover how differently they think and respond to one another's expectations.

"When we came across this guide for premarital counseling which Randall had written, we were eager to put it to use. We found it to be extremely helpful in preparing couples as they thought through their upbringing, expectations, challenges and dreams for building their new life together. The book, centered on Scripture, is practical, thorough and thought provoking.

"The couples learned much about each other as they eagerly worked through the 'homework assignments.' If you were to ask any of the couples we worked with using this material, they would tell you it helped them tremendously to get off to a great start in their marriage as well as to navigate

tougher times. Not only would we recommend this to all couples planning to marry, but the topics and homework will strengthen existing marriages young and old."
—Wyndham and Jeanie Shaw, Boston

"We used this guidebook to help a couple as they were getting married this fall after our daughter and son-in-law went through it before they got married. We were happy to see how biblical, thorough and full of examples it was. Both the couple about to get married and my husband and I thought that this was an excellent guide to prepare a couple for marriage. We are glad to see that it will get in the hands of many more couples as it gets published and has a wider audience."
—Alan and Sherry Rouse, Atlanta

"We have used the material to do pre-marital counseling with dozens of couples. We have found it to be very useful in initiating helpful conversations with couples. We highly recommend the material for Christian pre-marriage counseling." —David and Peggy Malutinok, Atlanta

LEARNING TO LIVE AS ONE

A Workbook for Engaged Couples

Randall Alexander

www.ipibooks.com

Learning to Live As One
©2023 by Illumination Publishers International.

All rights reserved.
No part of this book may be duplicated, copied, translated, reproduced or stored mechanically or electronically without specific, written permission of Illumination Publishers International.

All Scripture quotations, unless indicated, are taken from the NEW INTERNATIONAL VERSION.
Copyright ©1973, 1978, 1984 by the International Bible Society.
Used by permission of Zondervan Publishing House.
All rights reserved.

The "NIV" and "New International Version" trademarks are registered in the United States Patent Trademark Office by the International Bible Society.
Use of either trademarks requires the permission of the International Bible Society.

ISBN: 978-1-941988-12-1.

Cover Design: Brian Branch
Interior Design: Thais Gloor

Contents

Notes to Engaged Couples and to Mentoring Couples 6

Welcome: Getting Ready 7

Chapter 1: What Are My Expectations of Marriage? 11

Chapter 2: The Parents 14

Chapter 3: The Heart of the Matter 20

Chapter 4: Communication 34

Chapter 5: Making Decisions 43

Chapter 6: Resolving Conflict 50

Chapter 7: How Will You Spend Your Money? 60

Chapter 8: A Man and a Woman 70

Chapter 9: The Two Will Become One 75

Chapter 10: A Good Start 83

Note to Engaged Couples

The workbook is most useful when both of you have your own copy of the book, fill out the questions independently and then get together to discuss your answers. However, the workbook can help you prepare for marriage if you, alone, read the material and answer the questions. Most couples find it best to seek out a couple who can mentor them as they work through the material in the book. The workbook will reveal a lot about you, your future spouse and the areas where you may need help. A mentoring couple can provide more insight and can help you address things that surface as you work through the material.

Note to Mentoring Couples

This couple chose you to help them prepare to get married. Here are some suggestions based on our experience.

For most couples, about eight 1.5 hour sessions are required to complete the material included in this book. Set up time to meet together on a regular basis, usually once a week. This gives them time to prepare and spreads out the training to minimize the burden on their schedule. You can start as soon as the couple is engaged. Beginning the material 4 months in advance allows weeks to be missed when your schedules cannot be aligned and provides extra time to work on issues that need more time to address. If you get a late start, do your best to cover the material while being considerate of their schedule and your schedule. Chapter 9 usually is better when covered within a week or two of the wedding. All the other chapters can be done as soon as you can get time together.

Before you meet for a session have the couple:

1. Read the material
2. Fill out the questions
3. Discuss their answers together

Couples who want help to prepare for marriage generally do the assignment without much prompting. If couples do not take the time to read the chapter and respond to each other, then the session should be postponed until they have the time they need.

During a session, go over the answers to the questions rotating so that each gets a chance to answer a question first. The questions are designed to expose the areas in their relationship where they need some help. Feel free to ask other questions when you come to one of those areas. Give them the help they need to address the issue. Share with them how you have dealt with that issue or a similar one. Share some of the areas in your marriage that are difficult. Be open with them and be real. It is important for them to know that every marriage has its challenges. How we cope with them determines the strength or weakness of our relationship.

Do not attempt to go over every page in a chapter during a session. Use the questions to guide you in what to cover and where to spend your time. At least half the battle is discovering potential areas of trouble. Couples will often recognize them as they think through their answers and discuss them. Help the couple to feel at ease in asking *any* question, and use their answers to guide you as to where to spend your time.

More specific instructions for using this material to mentor an engaged couple can be found as an inexpensive purchase and download on the DPI Web site at www.dpibooks.org. The title of the material is *Learning to Live As One: A Mentor's Guide*. More information and updates are offered at www.learningtoliveasone.com.

Welcome

Getting Ready

So you have decided to get married. Congratulations! You have taken a big step, one that will affect the rest of your life. It is great to know that God cares about you and that he has been working to bring about what you need. He wants to give you the desires of your heart and to prosper you.

Psalm 20:4
*May he give you the desire of your heart
and make all your plans succeed.*

Jeremiah 29:11
*"For I know the plans I have for you," declares the Lord,
"plans to prosper you and not to harm you,
plans to give you hope and a future."*

How did the two of you meet?

_____

_____

_____

_____

_____

What attracted you to your companion?

_____

_____

_____

_____

_____

These fond memories will be shared with others over and over again. It is wonderful to be in love!

Ecclesiastes 4:9–12
*Two are better than one, because they have a good return for their work:
If one falls down, his friend can help him up.
But pity the man who falls and has no one to help him up!
Also, if two lie down together, they will keep warm. But how can one keep warm alone?
Though one may be overpowered, two can defend themselves.
A cord of three strands is not quickly broken.*

God's Blueprint for Marriage

God's plan for marriage is marvelous! He intended for this joy to last a lifetime and provided instructions so that you can find and keep this joy.

Marriage can also produce great pain. More than five out of every ten marriages in the U.S. end in divorce, most within the first seven years. The heartache, hurt feelings, resentment, fighting and trauma associated with each broken marriage will sober anyone contemplating this commitment. Personal experience with the pain of failed marriages can cause one to develop a deeply cynical and critical view of male-female relationships.

Thankfully, marriage, a centerpiece of God's creation, still rewards those who follow his blueprint. In marriage, just as in building a house, starting with all the right materials does not ensure success. The philosophy, "When you are in love, just let nature take its course," though common, rapidly brings disappointment, disillusionment and eventually failure. No one hires a contractor to build a house and tells him, "Just let nature take its course." We expect him to follow a blueprint that meets our approval. Similarly, those who follow God's plan can build a successful marriage that demonstrates the wisdom of God and shines like a light to a world that doubts such marriages exist.

Do not be misled. Great marriages do not result from finding just the right person with all the qualities you want in a mate, though finding the right partner is important. They do not come through careful pairing, though compatibility is important. Great marriages result from commitment and hard work. There are no shortcuts. So before you say your vows, work through the material in this book. It will help you prepare to get married.

Finally, seek out a mature godly couple that both of you respect and can relate to. Ask them to mentor your relationship and to spend time helping you get ready for marriage. Read the material one chapter at a time, and fill out the questions, each of you by yourself. Later, sit down together with your spouse-to-be and talk about your answers. Then get together with the mentoring couple you have chosen and go over your answers.

Read all the scriptures, answer all the questions fully and be open to change. Preparation for marriage builds character, matures you, and, in general, equips you for life. Be confident in the success that God promises to those who follow his blueprint. Put God at the center of your plans, commit your plans to him and he will bring about success.

Proverbs 16:3
Commit to the Lord whatever you do,
and your plans will succeed.

The selection of your life companion is a crucial choice. You do not want to make a mistake. The winds of emotion that accompany falling in love, though normal, hamper your ability to think logically. Get advice from people who know you and who have a mature relationship with God. Find mature godly couples who can give you the advice you need to succeed. Never is there a time in your life when you more desperately need sound advice.

Proverbs 15:22
Plans fail for lack of counsel,
but with many advisers they succeed.

How Compatible Are We?

While it may seem a bit late to look at compatibility, sooner is always better than later. Take a few moments and answer the following questions. They will help you to take a more unbiased look your relationship. Your answers will help the mentoring couple to see some of the challenges you will face and how they can best help you. Be open to godly advice. If a number of spiritually mature people have significant concerns about your relationship, take a step back and consider carefully what is being said. Other people can help you to be more objective. Strong feelings, especially love, can blind us to facts that are obvious to others.

Why do I want to marry this man or this woman?

1. _____
2. _____
3. _____
4. _____
5. _____

What makes us compatible? What common interests do we share? What do we like to do together?

1. _____
2. _____
3. _____
4. _____
5. _____
6. _____
7. _____
8. _____

How does my spouse-to-be bring out the best in me spiritually? What does he/she do that brings me closer to God? Since I began this relationship, in what ways have I grown spiritually and matured as a person?

1. _____
2. _____
3. _____

4. _____

5. _____

How do I help to bring out the best in my companion, spiritually and otherwise?

1. _____

2. _____

3. _____

4. _____

5. _____

Individually I have weaknesses that are strengthened when we are together. Make a list of those below.

Alone I am _____ together we are _____

Alone I am _____ together we are _____

Alone I am _____ together we are _____

Alone I am _____ together we are _____

Alone I am _____ together we are _____

What do others see in my life that demonstrates that I am at my best and a happier person when we are together?

1. _____

2. _____

3. _____

4. _____

5. _____

Proverbs 16:9
*In his heart a man plans his course,
but the Lord determines his steps.*

Proverbs 19:21
*Many are the plans in a man's heart,
but it is the Lord's purpose that prevails.*

1

What Are My Expectations of Marriage?

Goal: To develop realistic expectations for our marriage.

Love Never Fails (1 Corinthians 13:8)

Even the best marriages cannot meet fairy-tale expectations. Meals must be cooked, dishes washed, groceries bought and a living earned. Frequent compromises must be forged when his way does not match her way. Conflicts and hurt feelings must be resolved. Disappointments, bad days, sickness and sometimes, even tragedy must be faced. These challenges come to all marriages, both good and bad. Successful couples learn to face life together by drawing strength from each other. Realistic expectations, not delusions of "happily ever after," will prepare you to begin your marriage with hope, even optimism, as you face tomorrow's challenges. You can build a solid marriage that will be filled with joy, excitement and satisfaction. Life, with all it brings, can be fun as you live it to the full.

John 10:10b
I have come that they may have life, and have it to the full.

Love Is Commitment, Not Just Feelings

Love, as most people use the word, generally means that I have a strong feeling of attraction for you. "We fell in love. He knocked me off my feet; it was love at first sight." A husband attempting to explain his affair with another woman says, "We did not *intend* to fall in love." These feelings, though powerful and moving, cannot provide the primary basis for a relationship because they will change over time, sometimes suddenly. They can be directed toward you today and someone else tomorrow.

Love, as the Bible uses the word, nearly always means commitment. The Greek word *agape*, the word used in the love passage, 1 Corinthians 13:1–8, communicates decision and commitment to do the right thing. Love is patient and kind without envy, without boasting and without being proud, rude or selfish. It keeps no record of wrong. These beautiful words describe how each of us would like to be treated. The "love" qualities are difficult to practice and may even seem unnatural to you. Realizing them requires that you constantly deny your instincts, your natural desires, even your very self. This type of love never fails.

God Cares About Commitment and Feelings

God understands people and he understands marriage. He knows about feelings and commitment. He knows the importance of both! In Mark 12:30 the Message Bible reads, "So love the Lord God with all your passion and prayer and intelligence and energy." God wants us to love him with our heart, the center of our passion, as well as our intellect, our mind, where we understand and make long term commitments. This then teaches us how to love each other.

Commitment without the feelings will not satisfy. Feelings without commitment will not last. God planned for husbands and wives to have both types of love: commitment and attraction/desire for their mates.

Describe what you can imagine a typical day in your marriage to be.

_____
_____
_____
_____

Describe what you can imagine a bad day in your marriage will be.

_____
_____
_____
_____

What will be your greatest challenge in the marriage?

_____
_____
_____
_____

Ponder what many couples say in their vows during their wedding ceremony: "for better or worse, richer or poorer, in sickness or in health, and so on." What are some difficult things that could happen to your marriage?

_____
_____
_____
_____

Are you ready to fulfill your marriage vows? _____

Additional thoughts, questions and insights...

2

The Parents

Goal: To objectively look at our parents and their relationships to see both the positive and the negative. To help me gain insight to better understand my future mate and myself.

God provides very specific instructions for the role of the parents of a new couple. He repeats these words several times in the Bible to help us to understand the importance of them.

Genesis 2:24
*For this reason a man will leave his father and mother and be united to his wife,
and they will become one flesh.*

God simply says to "leave your parents." God is not talking about where you live. He is talking about your relationship with your parents after you are married. While it sounds simple, the process of leaving your parents can be quite involved, even for people who left home years ago. Not surprisingly, parents and family comprise one of the major sources of conflict in marriages.

An Acorn Does Not Fall Far from the Tree

Luke 6:40
*A student is not above his teacher,
but everyone who is fully trained will be like his teacher.*

While each of you can see some traits in yourself that you received from your parents, neither of you realizes the extent of your parents' impact on your life. Many fail to grasp the strong connection between their parents and the person they have become. Your biological parents supplied your DNA, all of the traits and characteristics associated with your body. Your parents, those who raised you, determined much of your environment during your formative years. Almost everyone stays in some form of communication with their parents after they leave home. Like it or not, your parents had, and continue to have, a profound impact on you. It is helpful to further understand this impact. In a sense, you do not know where you are going until you know where you have come from.

Every marriage brings at least two models into the relationship and no two are the same. One is her family and the other is his family. Though you may not understand why, you carry within you the tendency to be like your parents. What they did feels comfortable. When you visit with or talk about your in-laws-to-be, remember that your partner carries the tendency to do the things you see and hear. Be careful how you use this information. As you see your partner do the things they hate in their parents, do not say *or think*, "You are just like your father/mother!" This is irritating, hurtful and inflammatory. Rather, use the information to understand the struggles they are facing. Appreciate the difficulty they face and be assured that you will face similar temptations.

What strengths have you observed in your parents?

Mother

1 _____
2 _____
3 _____
4 _____

Father

1 _____
2 _____
3 _____
4 _____

What weaknesses have you observed in your parents?

Mother

1 _____
2 _____
3 _____
4 _____

Father

1 _____
2 _____
3 _____
4 _____

What strengths have you observed in your companion's parents?

Mother

1 _____
2 _____
3 _____
4 _____

Father

1 _____
2 _____
3 _____
4 _____

What weaknesses have you observed in your companion's parents?

Mother

1 _____
2 _____
3 _____
4 _____

Father

1 _____
2 _____
3 _____
4 _____

What strengths and weaknesses have you observed in your parents' marriage(s)?

Mother	Father
1 _____	1 _____
2 _____	2 _____
3 _____	3 _____
4 _____	4 _____

What strengths and weaknesses have you observed in the marriage(s) of your companion's parents?

Mother	Father
1 _____	1 _____
2 _____	2 _____
3 _____	3 _____
4 _____	4 _____

Describe the relationship you want to have with your future in-laws.

_____

_____

_____

In building that relationship with your in-laws-to-be, what do you think will be the greatest challenges?

_____

_____

_____

_____

How do you plan to make the relationship a good one? What are you doing now to achieve this goal?

_____

_____

_____

Now That I'm an Adult

As children grow up, parents must change from being parents to being peers. Many parents never make this difficult transition. They do not respect the adulthood of their children. Some are naïve, some are selfish, and some are both. They seek to maintain a strong parental influence on their children. Unable to just tell them what to do, these parents seek other more subtle ways to persuade their children. Grown children still possess a healthy desire to please their parents. Knowingly or not, some parents exploit that desire to manipulate their children. Some parents attempt to control by seeking pity and sympathy for their "poor" mother or father. Other parents use their intimate knowledge of their children's insecurities to obtain what they want. All of this can be accomplished while their children continue to view them as some of the most loving, caring parents on the planet.

Honor and respect your parents. Listen to their advice and wisdom. Talk to others who respect God's word and practice it. Then make your decisions. Some decisions you make will disappoint your parents. Since your spouse comes before your parents, you will not be able to accommodate them on some occasions. Unfortunately, these times will often be the holidays; one couple cannot always please two sets of parents.

Holidays and special occasions are important to your parents. Plan ahead. Sit down together, just the two of you, and come to agreement on what days you will spend with each of your families. Then communicate your joint decision to your parents. Seek to develop a way to share the holidays between your two families as fairly as possible. Most parents will be satisfied when they know what to expect and believe you considered their interest.

Generally speaking, bringing your parents into disagreements with your mate will not be helpful. Since most parents are not objective, engaging your parents in discussions about the faults of your mate will be unproductive. Sometimes, it will even be harmful. Parents tend to take your side, and that is not what you need when you have a disagreement with your spouse.

Bad attitudes toward your parents or your family will harm you and your marriage, even if you are not aware that these attitudes exist. The harmful effects can be complicated, subtle and often hard to identify without an understanding of your relationship with your parents. If you have even a slightly negative attitude toward your parents, or if others suspect you do, please take the time to explore what you feel and get help to resolve it. The future benefit to your marriage will be well worth your effort.

How often do you spend time with or talk to your parents? _____

What happens now when you say no to your parents' demands? Give an example.

_____

_____

_____

_____

In what areas do your parents typically provide you with advice?

Mother   Father

1. _____   1. _____

2. _____   2. _____

3. _____   3. _____

4. _____   4. _____

Do you owe your parents money? _____   If so, how much? _____

Do you have feelings of resentment toward your parents or any other members of your family? Is it difficult for you to discuss your relationship with anyone in your family? Do you have strained relations with anyone in your family? Do you dislike anyone in your family?

_____

_____

_____

_____

Additional thoughts, questions and insights...

3

The Heart of the Matter

Goal: To learn how to develop needed characteristics to produce a great marriage.

Before looking at communication, let us take a look at the heart of the matter. Your communication reflects what is in your heart. If your heart is right, then your communication will flow. If your heart is not right, then no adjustment or change in your mechanics can fix it.

Matthew 12:34b
For out of the overflow of the heart the mouth speaks.

The quality of your marriage depends on one thing more than any other. It is not compatibility, financial success, good looks, sexual attraction, good health or even how much you are in love! This one thing, more than all those combined, will determine the fate of your marriage. What is this one thing? It is your character, your ability to be like Christ. And it is all about your heart.

Prepare your heart now. Developing these character traits of Jesus allows God to bless your marriage. Without these principles many situations are a bump or disagreement waiting to happen. Each of these character traits can be attained to a high degree over time. None of them will come easily. Do not skip over these quickly. How well you practice these qualities will make or break your marriage. They are the crown jewels of relationships.

Jesus Empathized Strongly with Others

Empathy is the ability to put yourself in the place of another, to think what they think and to feel what they feel. Jesus knew how to do it well. He was always tuned in to what others thought and felt. In fact, he said that the Law and the Prophets could be summed up in one sentence: "Do to others as you would have them do to you" (Matthew 7:12). This cannot be done without putting yourself in their place.

Your ability to empathize, which is extremely important to the health of your relationship, allows you to truly share your joys and pain, to understand your mate and draw close to them. Empathy requires that you focus on what your mate is feeling and thinking by mentally putting yourself in their place.

Look at a few examples of how Jesus empathized with others:
1. Compassion on a hungry crowd – Mark 8:1–8
2. Concern for his mom while he was on the cross – John 19:26–27
3. Sympathy for the family of Lazarus – John 11:33–36

Try the following question to exercise your ability to empathize with another person. Read the clues, and use your intuition to figure out what the sinful woman and Simon are feeling and thinking about others in the story.

Read Luke 7:36–39. Think about Simon and the sinful woman.
What was the sinful woman feeling or thinking about...

Herself _____

Jesus _____

Simon _____

What was Simon feeling or thinking about...

Himself _____

Jesus _____

Sinful woman _____

Take a recent argument or disagreement that the two of you had. Tell the events from the other person's point-of-view (use "I" to refer to them) making their points about what they feel you did wrong. Be convincing!

_____

_____

_____

_____

_____

In what areas do you struggle to empathize with your companion?

_____

_____

_____

In what areas does your companion struggle to empathize with you?

_____

_____

_____

Challenge: "I will make every effort to put myself in my spouse's place and to attempt to understand what he/she thinks and feels." Yes _____ No _____

Jesus Humbled Himself

Philippians 2:6–8
Who, being in very nature God,
did not consider equality with God something to be grasped,
but made himself nothing,
taking the very nature of a servant,
being made in human likeness.
And being found in appearance as a man,
he humbled himself
and became obedient to death—
even death on a cross!

Jesus was completely humble, even in his decision to come to the earth. He shows us how to be humble. He came as God to the earth, yet he neither denied nor flaunted his position (John 18:37). When confronted, he did not become defensive or strike back (Luke 4:28–30, 20:1–8). He spoke confidently, but he did not sound like a know-it-all seeking to prove to how important he was (John 5:19). When complimented, he graciously accepted the praise (Luke 19:37–-40). When he corrected others he had a simple agenda: to help them. He never corrected others to make himself look better.

Why is humility so important to a marriage? Conflicts are nearly impossible to completely resolve without it.

Signs of pride
- I struggle to see my faults and shortcomings.
- I find it difficult to admit the problems I can see.
- I am convinced that the problems you think you find in me are misunderstandings and misjudgments.
- I promote myself and may not realize that in doing so, I put you down.
- I seek to show the problem is yours—at least, not mine—by proving that what I did was right and defensible, even though this process hurts you deeply.
- I like to believe I am better than I often appear to others.
- I am uncomfortable with compliments and may shrug them off or talk about how I could have done better.

Signs of humility
- You bring a problem to my attention, and I seek to understand the full extent of the problem.
- I am willing to see my faults and shortcomings without defending them.
- I am comfortable with my imperfect self, and I seek to find ways to build you up.
- I accept blame for the hurt I have caused.
- Seeing your hurt shows me why I should not have said or done what I did.
- Your perception of me helps me to understand my shortcomings.
- Your compliments build be up, and I express my appreciation for them

Psalm 36:2

*For in his own eyes he flatters himself
too much to detect or hate his sin.*

Pride and arrogance can be difficult to change. Here are some suggestions on how you can, with God's help, conquer them:
1. Pray about your sin and your desire to change.
2. Read scriptures that describe God's greatness as compared to yours (Job 38–39, Romans 9:19–21).
3. Ponder a couple of scriptures on humility (Colossians 3:12, 1 Peter 5:5).
4. Understand that your worth to God is not based on your accomplishments (Jeremiah 29:11, Matthew 10:29–30).
5. Understand grace (Ephesians 2:8–10, Romans 8:1–4).

Think of at least one example of Jesus demonstrating a humble response in a challenging situation.

_____

_____

_____

Why is humility so important to a marriage?

_____

_____

_____

Consider the following comments. For the two examples, answer the questions and suggest a humble response.

With an edge in her voice she says, "We never go out anymore! When we were single you always had interesting dates planned. You made me feel really special. Now, all we do is rent a movie or go for a burger. You are ashamed of me. That's why we never go on dates. Right?"

What is she feeling?

_____

_____

What does she need?

_____

_____

What is a humble response?

_____

_____

"You know how your mom is always finishing sentences for everyone. You have started doing that all the time. I can't say anything without you interrupting me to finish my thought. Do not ever do that again."

What is he feeling?

_____

_____

What does he need?

_____

_____

What is a humble response?

_____

_____

Discuss a recent situation in which you had a prideful response. Describe what you did and what you would have done if you had been humble. If you cannot remember a time when you have been prideful, discuss how you demonstrated humility during a recent situation.

_____

_____

_____

Challenge: "I have decided to make every effort to be completely humble in all circumstances, whether complimented or criticized, even when, at first, I cannot see the truth in the criticism."

Yes _____ No _____

Jesus Was Totally Unselfish

John 8:29
*"The one who sent me is with me; he has not left me alone,
for I always do what pleases him."*

It is interesting that being unselfish does not prevent Jesus from presenting his needs. In John 4 he asks for a drink of water. While on the cross he says that he is thirsty. Being unselfish does not mean that you never tell anyone what you need. It has everything to do with how you act when your needs are not met.

Unselfish people make requests for what they need and what they want. And they do not get upset if their request is denied. Selfish people make demands, disguised as requests. It sounds like a request unless it is refused. Then, because of the reaction, it becomes clear that it was a demand. Good marriages should be filled with requests. This means you must create an environment where it is okay to say no.

So make a decision now to be unselfish. Read Philippians 2:1–4. Decide to put your mate above yourself, and God will bless your marriage. In the end, your needs will get met in a far greater measure if you trust God and trust your mate enough to put their needs above your own.

Why was Jesus able to be so unselfish?

_____

_____

_____

When do you find it hardest for you to be unselfish, and how do you deal with these situations?

_____

_____

_____

When does your spouse-to-be find it hardest to be unselfish, and how do they deal with these situations?

_____

_____

_____

Challenge: "I will make every effort to be totally unselfish in all circumstances, even when it is hard and even when it seems that my needs are not getting met." Yes _____ No _____

Jesus Accepted People As They Are

Jesus, though he never sinned, achieved the distinction, "friend of sinners." Read the following scriptures, John 8:1–11, Luke 7:36–39, Luke 5:12–13, Mark 5:1–8. Jesus fully accepted the sick, the demon possessed and even blatant sinners. This drove the Pharisees crazy (Luke 5:30) because they considered themselves better than the sinners (Luke 18:11). They confused accepting them with approving their actions. Jesus understood that he could accept the person. In other words, he could approve of the person without approving their actions. Jesus told the sinful woman to "leave her life of sin" while he graciously and completely accepted her.

Marriage requires that you totally accept your mate. With only a few examples of extreme behavior like marital unfaithfulness and physical abuse, you agree to completely accept your mate when you marry. Perhaps you find it easy to agree with this point. You have picked this person because you want to totally accept them, as you want them to totally accept you.

When you begin living together, knowing that you plan to spend the rest of your life together, beware that flaws you never noticed in your mate can suddenly appear. It can be like moving into a house you thought was in good shape and suddenly noticing defects everywhere. You carefully inspected the house before moving in, but you never saw the defects. The realization that your mate has flaws that you never noticed can be scary.

Accepting your spouse does not mean just hanging around instead of leaving them. Accepting people as Jesus did begins in your heart. It means that you can learn to be content in your circumstances—even if they never change. Resentful tolerance does not work. Your mate will feel your resentment, and that will make it worse. Acceptance means getting comfortable with their flaws, excusing them and putting them in the very best light—just as you do with your flaws. And that, by the way, contrary to your intuition, is the very best thing you can do to help your spouse to change.

Women: How should you handle the following situation:

Your husband picks apart everything you do. He criticizes your clothes, your hair, your make-up, your cooking, the pictures on the wall, the furniture arrangement, your body and the way you treat him. Despite all efforts to persuade him to stop, he continues, believing that this is how he will help you to be your best.

_____

_____

_____

_____

Men: How should you handle the following situation:

Your wife becomes very unhappy. She gains thirty-five pounds and cries profusely whenever you talk to her about anything, especially her weight. Every discussion quickly turns into a listing of all your shortcomings. She bemoans your lack of encouragement, compliments and help around the house as she continues to cry. She describes the way you are hurting her in horrific terms that you thought were reserved for murder trials and the 11 o'clock news. She feels shortchanged by you and by life. Despite all your efforts to please her, nothing changes.

_____
_____
_____
_____

Do you think your mate will be able to tell if you just tolerated something but had not accepted it in your heart? How could they tell?

_____
_____
_____

Why is it so important to accept them from the heart, as they are, even if they never change?

_____
_____
_____
_____

What things could you NOT accept in your mate?

1. _____
2. _____
3. _____
4. _____
5. _____

How can you improve your ability to accept undesirable traits in your mate?
   1. Pray about it
   2. Empathize
   3. Realize their strengths
   4. Realize your weaknesses

Challenge: "I will make every effort to genuinely accept my spouse, good or bad, strengths or weaknesses, completely." Yes _____ No _____

Jesus Forgave People Completely

John 1:14
The Word became flesh and made his dwelling among us. We have seen his glory, the glory of the One and Only, who came from the Father, full of grace and truth.

1 Peter 4:8
Above all, love each other deeply, because love covers over a multitude of sins.

Jesus came to the earth to teach us how to live. He forgave so freely that John describes him as "full of grace and truth." Consider what it means to be full of grace, to have a never-ending supply of forgiveness. Despite the harsh treatment he received, he freely forgave the people who hurt him. He never focused on the wrong done to him, never retaliated, never grew resentful, never lapsed into self-pity, never harbored anger or bitterness in his heart, and never allowed the hurt he received from others to cause him to respond harshly.

Marriage will present you with many opportunities to forgive. Perhaps it was Peter, the married disciple, in Luke 17:5 who led the hopeless response, "Increase our faith!" when told to forgive anyone who came seven times and said, "I repent." Maybe Peter was thinking about the times his wife offended him and how difficult it was to forgive her.

The closer you get to each other in your marriage, the more vulnerable you become and the more easily your mate can hurt you, often unintentionally. Regardless of why they hurt you, you will have plenty of opportunities to forgive.

Forgiveness renews your marriage and keeps it pure and fresh. Your hurt feelings that remain unresolved, those for which you have not forgiven your mate, will make you bitter and spoil your marriage. Like rotten potatoes in your kitchen, until they are removed, they will affect everything around you. Learn to forgive like Jesus did, as you go, so that your relationship remains fresh and alive.

What hurt do you think was hardest for Jesus to forgive and why?

_____

_____

_____

Jesus forgave completely. How did this affect his ability to deal appropriately with others?

_____

_____

_____

How can you tell that you have completely forgiven? What would indicate that you have not forgiven completely?

_____

_____

_____

Consider a significant issue with your spouse-to-be where he/she hurt or bothered you in some way. Have you forgiven them? What indicators make you feel that you have or have not forgiven completely?

_____

_____

_____

Challenge: "I will make every effort to forgive my spouse completely, as I go." Yes _____ No _____

Jesus Loved Unconditionally

We find out about the love of God in Romans 8:38–39. The Bible tells us that nothing can separate us from the love of God. We know that Jesus shows us who God is in the flesh. He loved everyone regardless of how they treated him. Look at Luke 13:34. Jesus expresses his love for Jerusalem in terms of a mother taking care of her young. He loved them like a mother, in spite of their rejection of him.

As people, we need love most when we are at our worst. There are times in all of our lives when we get frustrated, discouraged or faithless. Love, at these times, helps us to improve our attitude and our behavior. In other words, the times your mate treats you the worst are the times they need your love the most. Of course, this is when it is hardest to give love. It will only happen if you have made a decision to love unconditionally, as Jesus loved, even if you are feeling rejected or hurt by them.

Give three examples, not listed above, that demonstrate the unconditional love of Jesus.

_____

_____

_____

In what situations or areas are you tempted to love your companion conditionally?

_____

_____

_____

In what situations or areas do you feel loved conditionally by your companion?

_____

_____

_____

Challenge: "I will make every effort to do what is best for my spouse in all situations, to love them unconditionally." Yes _____ No _____

Jesus Knew What to Think

Philippians 4:8

Finally, brothers, whatever is true, whatever is noble, whatever is right, whatever is pure, whatever is lovely, whatever is admirable—if anything is excellent or praiseworthy—think about such things.

Perhaps the greatest lesson you can learn from Jesus is how to think. Paul tells us here in Philippians to have the attitude of Christ. This word for "attitude," translated "mind" in the KJV, means literally "to exercise your mind." In other words, you need to learn to think like Jesus. Jesus rebukes Peter using this same Greek word in Matthew 16:23. "You are thinking the wrong way, exercising your mind for Satan not for God," Jesus tells him.

While on the cross, Jesus demonstrates in a powerful way how to use your mind. One of his seven recorded statements provides some insight into his way of thinking. He says, "Father, forgive them, for they do not know what they are doing" (Luke 23:34). The last half of that statement may actually seem strange to you when you think about it. Jesus puts himself in the place of the people who are abusing him, and he searches for a reason for their behavior. Forgiving people who act out of ignorance is much easier than forgiving people who are simply out to get you. Trying to think from the perspective of those who bring you harm helps you to forgive them. Your marriage will test how you think. Think the right things, and God will bless you beyond your imagination. Allow your mind to focus on the wrong things, and you will find marriage to be far less fulfilling and far more challenging than you thought it would be. The KJV says in Proverbs 23:7, "For as he thinketh in his heart, so is he." As you think in your heart, so will be your marriage. Consider the recommended thoughts for each of the following situations:

When you first wake up
- I am thankful for my companion.
- What does he/she need from me today?
- How can I build him/her up?
- How can I express affection to him/her that communicates my love?

When you separate for the day
- What is he/she doing today? Is today a special day?
- When can I talk to him/her today?
- How can I encourage him/her in their tasks?
- Does he/she know when to expect me home?

- What are our plans for the evening?
- Is there information I need to communicate to him/her?
- Do I need something from him/her today?
- Plan to hug and kiss him/her as you leave.

When you are coming home
- What has he/she been doing today?
- What will he/she be doing when I get home?
- What will he/she need me to do?
- Anticipate how you will give him/her a warm greeting.

When you arrive home
- How can I greet him/her warmly and express affection.
- What is he/she feeling; how did his/her day go?
- How can I help?
- What news can I share?

When you get ready for bed
- How can I express affection to him/her, (i.e., give a backrub or foot massage, hold each other)?
- Is it a good time to make love?
- How can I build him/her up?
- Express what he/she means to you.

When your spouse expresses hurt feelings
- What have I done to cause or contribute to the hurt?
- Why is he/she feeling this way; what is the connection to what I did?
- How has the hurt affected him/her?
- Do I now understand why he/she is hurting?
- Express what you hear from his/her point of view in your words, being careful not to minimize.

When your spouse feels down
- What is he/she feeling and why?
- How can I help him/her to talk about their feelings without offering a quick fix and without criticizing, listening only to understand what he/she is feeling and why?

When you feel hurt
- Can I forgive him/her for this?
- In other words—can I let this go, never to think or talk about it again?
- If not, when should I talk about my hurt feelings?
- Are there other factors that contributed to the way I feel (bad day, feeling sick, hurts from someone else or disappointments in myself)?
- He/she did not intend to hurt me this way. Assuming this is true, how could this have happened?
- Can I think of a scenario in which I have done the same wrong thing in a similar situation?

Some of these thoughts may seem strange or even wrong to you. If so, do not use this as a reason to ignore this way of thinking. Share how you feel and talk it through. Unselfish thinking, expressed in these situations, often seems unnatural, perhaps even unfair. Interestingly, we all want to be treated unselfishly. Unselfishness appeals to us and even seems right when we receive it. Thinking and behaving unselfishly, the key to a successful marriage and relationship, will happen when you decide to be like Jesus with conviction and determination.

Since no one knows exactly what you are thinking, why is what you think so important? (Hint: In Matthew 12:34, Jesus says, "For out of the overflow of the heart the mouth speaks.")

_____

_____

Consider the following situation: You have just expressed how your mate hurt you. In return, he/she angrily attacks you again. What thoughts would be helpful to you as you respond?

_____

_____

_____

_____

I have decided to show empathy, humility, unselfishness, acceptance, forgiveness, unconditional love to my spouse-to-be in the way that Jesus showed it to others and to think like Jesus would think in this relationship.

If you agree, sign your name here: _____

Rate your progress

Rate yourself and your companion on your effectiveness in these areas. (1 – very poor, 10 – awesome)

You		Your companion	
Empathy	_____	Empathy	_____
Humility	_____	Humility	_____
Unselfishness	_____	Unselfishness	_____
Acceptance	_____	Acceptance	_____
Forgiveness	_____	Forgiveness	_____
Unconditional love	_____	Unconditional love	_____
Think like Christ	_____	Think like Christ	_____

Additional thoughts, questions and insights...

4

Communication

Goal: To learn to establish good communication with my spouse.

Good communication to a marriage is like water to a plant. While a plant can survive for a time without water, eventually it will die. Over time you can look at a plant and tell whether or not it has been getting water. It will be lush and green, or it will be parched and dry. The same is true of a marriage. Over time a marriage will reflect the quality of its communication.

Good conversation starts with talking about what activities you will do today and continues to a deeper level: what you think, how you feel and why. What do you want the quality of your communication to be in your marriage? What are your goals? How will you get there? What will it take from you? Are you willing to learn and change your habits to obtain your goal?

Learn to Listen

James 1:19
*My dear brothers, take note of this: Everyone should be quick to listen,
slow to speak and slow to become angry.*

How well you listen will determine how well you communicate. While everyone listens every day, few do it well. A good listener makes their companion feel heard, loved, respected and valuable. Before you judge how well you listen, consider the following fundamentals of listening. Do yourself a favor: Learn to listen. The level of intimacy you share with your mate will be determined to a high degree by how well you listen.

1. **Bring the right mindset** – Move yourself into the background and focus on the speaker.
2. **Give your full attention** – Face them squarely and interact, making eye contact. Show interest.
3. **Draw them out** – Learn the words that draw them out and encourage them to talk more.

Proverbs 20:5
*The purposes of a man's heart are deep waters,
but a man of understanding draws them out.*

4. **Understand their reasoning** – Be able to make their case, convincingly, to someone else.
5. **Feel what they feel** – Notice their tone, inflection and body language. What are they feeling?
6. **Share what you hear in your own words** – Good communication requires feedback, in your own words.
7. **Let the Spirit guide you** – Be sensitive to where he leads you; he will help you to listen.

Why We Don't Listen

The world today, filled with busy lives, sets very low standards for listening. We feel some situations justify our not listening. We focus on a task or a problem to the exclusion of all else around us. We exhaust ourselves to the point that we think our brains are mush and incapable of listening. We feel that we have worked hard enough for the day, and we are ready only to be entertained by the TV or a movie. The list goes on and on. Even when we do hear the words that are said, often we do not really listen. Consider the following obstacles that prevent us from being a good listener, and think about how to overcome them.

1. **Not interested** – I have no interest in what you are saying.
2. **Easily distracted** – You said something that made me think of something else.
3. **My turn to talk** – I have more valuable things to share than what you are saying.
4. **I disagree** – When you make a mistake, I am ready to set it right with persuasive facts, figures and arguments. I enjoy a good argument. It helps me to learn and communicate.
5. **The fix-it shop** – I listen because I know how to help. I can tell you how to fix your problem.
6. **Judge and jury** – Every conversation is a chance for me to rule on what you did or said.

Which of these obstacles to listening tempts you the most? How often?

_____

_____

_____

Which of these obstacles to listening most tempts your spouse-to-be? How often?

_____

_____

_____

Read the following story and <u>underline</u> what he did right. Though the story is written about a male listening to a female, it applies both ways.

His friend on the phone made him laugh again, just as his wife walked into the house. He noticed her taut face, the glare in her eyes and her stiff but quick walk. Clearly, she was upset as she returned from her mother's house. He ended the phone call, lost the smile from his face, and patiently waited for her to speak. Though he wanted to tell her about the award he received at work today, he decided now was not a good time. He began to think about what might have happened between her and her mom. He remembered their recent decision to spend her birthday at home rather than go to her mom's as she always had in the past.

He sat solemnly for a couple of minutes waiting for her to speak. Then he said, "What happened?"
She said, "I don't want to talk about it."
"Is your mom upset?" he asked.
"She makes me so mad. She still thinks I am five years old," she continued. She talked for the next five minutes, pausing only for an occasional response from him: "Oh," "Hmm," "Really," and "that must have been hard."
He resisted his urge to point out where she had been wrong and to suggest another approach. Before she finished, she began to feel bad about the way she had treated her mom. She finished with, "It must be hard for Mom to miss my birthday for the first time. I am going to call and apologize to her. Honey, you have been so helpful. Thanks."
"You're welcome," was all that he said before telling her his good news.

What can you learn from the man in the story?

_____
_____
_____
_____

Couples Need to Talk
What is the purpose of talking in your marriage; what do you hope to accomplish?

1. _____   5. _____
2. _____   6. _____
3. _____   7. _____
4. _____   8. _____

Married couples need to talk, beginning with chit-chat. Small talk plays an important role in communication. Like warm-ups before exercise, light conversation helps a couple to move into heavier topics. Everyone can learn to do this, but some couples need more help than others. Interacting with another couple can be helpful. Observe how they talk to each other, and ask them how you can improve conversation between the two of you. No heavy emotion and no heavy topics allowed, just chat.

Keep it light and informative. Think about twenty minutes a day as a minimum. Fight for this time. Use the phone if that is the only way to make it happen. Even when you travel out of town, you can talk via cell phone or long distance to keep each other informed. See a sample of suggested topics listed below:

Morning (Breakfast)
- What are your plans for the day?
- What are your plans for this evening?
- Do you have any major events today?
- (Current events) What do you think?
- When will you be home?
- What do you want or need from me today?
- What do I want or need from you?

Spiritual
- Thought from your time with God

Dinner
- How was your day; what happened?
- What did I do today?
- Did you have any significant conversations?
- Did I?
- Were there any surprises?
- What are your plans for the evening?
- What do you want or need from me?

Spiritual
- Temptations today

Go Deeper: Share your feelings

One of the most exciting aspects of marriage is the opportunity to know and to be completely known by another person. God showed us the pattern for great relationships. He knows us (Matthew 10:29–30), and he wants us to know him (John 15:14, Acts 17:27). This never happens by accident. Knowing requires curiosity, inquiry and the interest to remember and digest. Being known requires the willingness to reveal yourself to another, to tell them everything about you, including how you think and how you feel. Because others in their past may have used this information for harm, many find it difficult to reveal their inner self, even to their mate. Some may fear that their mate might run away if they knew the ugly truths they keep locked inside. However, over time we learn to share our inmost feelings.

Genesis 2:24
For this reason a man will leave his father and mother and be united to his wife, and they will become one flesh.

Becoming one flesh means that, in marriage, you commit to share everything. Though sharing everything may sound easy, most couples find it challenging. Do not be discouraged if your attempts to practice this fall short of your expectations. This process takes time. Open your heart to your spouse. Learn to share what you think and feel about everything. If you have trouble sharing how you feel toward each other, start by sharing how you feel about other things.

All people experience feelings, but their approach to their feelings varies widely. With regard to understanding what they feel, most men and women enter marriage at very different levels; women usually understand their feelings better. Further, they enter with different levels of comfort in talking about their feelings; women usually feel more comfortable. Consider the following examples.

"How are you feeling?" she said, hoping to find out more about his inner thoughts on the subject.
"Fine," her spouse replied, with a blank expression that revealed nothing to her. He could not understand her preoccupation with always wanting to know how he felt.
"Why won't you let me inside? You always push me away," she said, now both upset and hurt. Women, he thought, were not made to be understood.

What could she have said or done that might have been more helpful?

_____

_____

_____

> She said, "I do not feel good about this," as she nervously scanned the downtown hotel.
>
> "Why?" he asked, seeking a valid explanation for her hesitation, being especially aware of the time and money they had already invested in this getaway.
>
> "I don't know, but I just do not feel good about it," she repeated, this time with much stronger conviction.
>
> "Sometimes I just wish you would keep your feelings to yourself," he said, as he pondered what to do next. He felt that their money had been wasted and his plans for the special weekend had been ruined.

What could he have said to her that may have been more helpful?

_____

_____

_____

In general, men and women process feelings differently as you can see in the examples above. Women often have trouble understanding why men are so hesitant to share their feelings, and men often fail to understand why women want to talk about feelings. It takes time to develop our ability to communicate about our feelings so that we can understand each other. In the following exercise let your mind free-associate as you consider how you feel about different things. This exercise will be trivial for some and challenging for others. Learn the language of feelings and open up your heart (2 Corinthians 6:11–13).

Some Words Used to Communicate Feelings

Happy	Sad	Disappointed	Angry	Hurt (feelings)	Embarrassed
Upset	Worried	Excited	Anxious	Overwhelmed	Confused
Proud	Close	Apathetic	Depressed	Sorry	Empty
Satisfied	Content	Confident	Afraid	Attacked	Unhappy
Pumped	Bored	Challenged	Grateful	Dread	Opposed

Pick the word that best describes how you feel about the following subjects.

_____ My job

_____ My relationship with God

_____ Our plans for the wedding

_____ My relationship with my dad

_____ My ability to be a great husband/wife

_____ Our national economy

_____ Watching TV

_____ My relationship with my mom

_____ What I have accomplished in my life

_____ The car I drive

_____ Where I live or will live

_____ My education

_____ The death penalty

_____ My childhood

Feelings are not always rational or reasonable, but they are real. Do not spend time arguing with feelings or judging feelings. Don't say, "You should not feel that way." Or "It is not right to feel that way." Or "I do not think that is how you really feel." Listen, seek to understand the feelings you hear expressed, and accept them. Make your home a safe place where hearts can be open without the fear of attack or judgmental put-downs.

Body Language

Try the following exercise with a friend (not your spouse-to-be). Say, "I'd love to go with you" three times, each time communicating a different message. Have them try to determine what you intend to communicate and record their answers.

Words	**Implied Message**	**Received Message**
1. I'd love to go with you.	That is the last thing on earth I want to do.	_____
2. I'd love to go with you.	I can't wait to go with you.	_____
3. I'd love to go with you.	I'll go but I'm not sure I have the time.	_____

How accurately did they receive the implied messages?

_____

_____

Seek to communicate in words rather than tone and body language. Words provide the most effective way to navigate the emotional rapids of life. With practice you can use words to steer your way into and out of highly charged topics without sinking your boat. Tone and body language lack precision and often transmit inaccurate and confusing messages.

Why is body language not a preferred way to get your message across?

_____

_____

Notice that you communicate in two ways: what you say and how you say it. From the exercise you can see that how we say it is more heavily weighted than what we say. How you say it also has two components: what you do with your voice (tone) and what you do with your body (body language). How you say what you say is important. It provides a window to your heart and to what you are feeling.

Matthew 12:34b
For out of the overflow of the heart the mouth speaks.

Since your heart will be displayed in your tone and your body language, get your heart right! Do not underestimate the importance of what you think and how you feel about a topic. Try as you might, you can never keep it fully concealed.

Why does your body language matter when you talk with your mate?

_____

_____

_____

Learn How to React

From an early age we learned to ask, "Who started it?" The guilty party always got the most severe punishment, and the victim received more grace, or at least a lighter punishment. This principle sometimes can help to sort out conflicts between children. However, in marriage, it is often used to justify or excuse vindictive behavior between adults. And do you really know who started it? Consider the following story.

In his haste to go out and play, a large, gangly five-year-old unknowingly knocks down a smaller classmate, scraping the skin off both his knees. The injured little boy jumps up and kicks his unsuspecting five-year-old attacker in the shins producing a large bruise. Immediately the five-year-old pushes the little boy down into the mud. Stop. When asked who started the spat, each pointed at the other, believing with all their heart that the other had started the fight.

What can you learn from this story about how to react to your mate?

_____

_____

_____

This story illustrates how arguments and disagreements often start. Misunderstandings, accidents and untimely circumstances often strike the first blow. Our reactions intensify; sometimes even create the conflict. Because we blame everything on the offending party, we can feel fully justified while verbally striking blow after blow, purposefully aiming to hurt. Reaction, or more aptly put, retaliation, almost always causes more pain than the first offense. Further, retaliation escalates conflict, increasing the harm and the risk. A godly response averts conflict.

James 1:19–20
My dear brothers, take note of this: Everyone should be quick to listen, slow to speak and slow to become angry, for man's anger does not bring about the righteous life that God desires.

Slow to speak and slow to become angry means slow to react. Be quick to listen. Be eager to understand and to discover the reason you felt attacked. Before you embrace the common notion, "Because they wanted to hurt me," think deeper. Give the offender the benefit of the doubt. Be quick to overlook the offenses that come your way and learn to forgive quickly. Leave vengeance to God, the only accurate judge. Guard your heart, your spirit and your reactions. Willingly accept blame for the hurt you caused by your *reaction*. Do not justify what you do by what was done to you.

Why is it important to be slow to react? Generally, how quickly do you react?

_____

_____

_____

Think before you act. Do whatever it takes even if it means counting to 10 or 100. Reactions are not like reflexes. You do have a choice. It lies between what happens to you and what you do.

What happens to you ⟶ | Your choice | ⟶ What you do

Additional thoughts, questions and insights...

5

Making Decisions

Goal: To learn to make decisions with my spouse that are mutually satisfying.

Decisions, decisions—how many there are to make. When you make them all yourself, you hardly notice them. When decisions involve two parties with different interests, the decisions become not only more noticeable but also more challenging. At first, before you establish some patterns, even the smallest decisions can take considerable time to resolve. A successful conclusion to a decision-making conversation means that you and your mate feel good about (1) each other and (2) the resulting decision or the decision to discuss it at a later time.

List of Decisions to Consider

Domestic
- When to get up?
- When to go to bed?
- When to eat meals?
- What food to buy, cook and eat?
- Who will cook, clean, take out the garbage and maintain the house?
- How will you decorate?
- Schedule of activities.
- Selection of furniture.
- How clean and neat?
- Company over? When?
- Where to live?

Family
- Where to spend Christmas?
- Where to spend Thanksgiving?
- When to call?
- Visits here/there? How long?
- Any family events?
- Presents?

Job
- Continue in same job?
- Number of hours?
- Amount of travel?
- Impact on family?
- Socialize with job friends?
- Potential realized?
- Money enough?

Entertainment
- Special dates? When?
- Together? Apart? When?
- Hobbies? How much time?
- Pets? What kind? How many?
- Which movies? TV shows? Sports?
- Read books? When?

Money
- Budget? Regular reviews?
- Maximum individual purchase?
- Veto power? How does it work?
- Gifts? How much?
- Cars, house, maintenance?
- Investments? How to decide? Reviewing?
- Entertainment? How much?

Religion/Church
- Involved in which activities?
- Morality of decisions/activities?
- Contribution. How much?

For too many of us, interacting with our family and friends taught us how not to make decisions. Too often, decision-making sessions involve manipulation, intimidation, selfishness, arrogance, shouting, crying fake tears and total emotional shut down. Will it be her way or his way or no way?

Good decision making discussions leave both of you feeling valued and respected. Even when you did not get what you want, you can feel good about the decision because you know why you *voluntarily* sacrificed getting what you want. Bad decision-making discussions will leave you feeling anxious, insecure, guilty or maybe used. Even when you get what you want, you may not feel good about it.

What best describes your tendency?

____ I shut down in disagreements.

____ I give in rather than argue.

____ I will give up something if you will.

____ I seek to convince you to do what I want.

What best describes your companion's tendency?

____ I shut down in disagreements.

____ I give in rather than argue.

____ I will give up something if you will.

____ I seek to convince you to do what I want.

Name a time when you...

Gave in to your spouse-to-be. _____

Your spouse-to-be gave in to you. _____

You compromised. _____

Could not discuss with your spouse-to-be. _____

Effective decision-making requires a 3-D process: Discovery, Discussion and Decision. The first step allows you to gather the information you need to make the decision. The second step provides a chance for each to react to the other's wants and needs. The last step, of course, is where the two of you make the decision.

Discovery Phase

Decision-making should include the following simple facts for each person:
1. What is the question, the decision to be made? A clear statement of the issue.
2. What does each of you want? This must be clear, no hidden agendas.
3. Why do you want this? Explain why, do not assume.
4. How strongly do you care about the outcome? How much does it matter? How does it impact you?

Fill out the following chart on your own for six different important decisions:

1. What time will the two of you go to bed?
Time: _____
Why: _____
How much you care (1-None, 10-Much) ___

2. What time will the two of you get up?
Time: _____
Why: _____
How much you care (1-None, 10-Much) ___

3. Who will take out the garbage?
Who: _____
Why: _____
How much you care (1-None, 10-Much) ___

4. Unplanned maximum individual buy?
$: _____
Why: _____
How much you care (1-None, 10-Much) ___

5. Where will you spend Christmas?
Where: _____
Why: _____
How much you care (1-None, 10-Much) ___

6. Where will you spend Thanksgiving?
Where: _____
Why: _____
How much you care (1-None, 10-Much) ___

Pitfalls During the Discovery Phase
1. Reacting negatively to your companion's wants, even with body language
2. Asking for more than you want for additional "bargaining power"
3. Not sharing what you want for fear that it will be rejected
4. Feeling that your companion's request cannot be refused
5. Spending your time figuring out how you will get what you want

When we discuss a decision, my companion knows what I want:

Always ___   Almost always ___   Usually ___   Sometimes ___   Rarely ___   Never ___

Discussion Phase

Once you have all the information, you are ready to discuss the matter. Read Amos 3:3, 1 Corinthians 1:10 and Philippians 2:1–4 and refer to them often. Make agreement your goal. Agreement means simply that both of you agree that the resulting decision is the best one for the two of you right now. It does not mean that you have the same logic, reasoning or moral judgments.

Some approach the discussion phase as an opportunity to prove that what they want is the only conclusion a thinking, moral person with any common sense would do. This thinking is arrogant and foolish. Not only does it call for your spouse to do what you want, it requires that they agree with your logic, reasoning and precise moral judgments. In the end, this behavior seeks to avoid the essence of decision making, essentially saying what you want and asking another to submit to your desires.

Decisions about what color to paint a room, where to place furniture and whether or not to eat between meals are not moral decisions. Be careful not to turn matters of opinion into discussions of morals, ethics or logic. The Bible does not tell us how much money to spend on a present or what to eat. It does not tell us what furniture to buy. Multiple points of view can lead to better decision making. Pool your thinking to become wiser. Be willing to be persuaded. Imagine doing exactly what your spouse has purposed and thinking about how to make it work, not just what is wrong with it. Fully consider their point of view even if they do not consider yours.

Continue to talk it through when it seems difficult to make progress. Try another angle. How can we make this work? Assume that a solution exists that would be mutually agreeable. You may have to give up more than you would like. Both of you may have to give up more than you would like. But a solution exists. Find it.

Consider the reciprocal principle. If you are feeling something, there is a good chance that they feel it, too. If you feel they are being unreasonable, they may feel you are being unreasonable. If you feel they are being selfish, they may feel you are. If you feel they are angry with you, they may feel you are angry with them. If you feel attacked, they may feel attacked as well. The reciprocal principle often rings true and nearly always leads you to productive thoughts.

Pitfalls During the Discussion Phase
1. Not listening to your mate's reasoning and requests
2. Focused only on what you want
3. Dramatic presentation of your side
4. Raising your voice
5. Using inflammatory words (i.e., you always, you never, that would be stupid, you are selfish)
6. Attacking your mate, insults
7. Shutting down, saying, "whatever you want"
8. Crying manipulative tears

Decision Phase
1. Learn to be decisive. Sometimes, because of time, you are forced to decide quickly. Even no decision may be a decision. Grow to the point that the discussion can be, "We can do what you want." "No, we can do what *you* want." Trust that God will take care of you, even when you are unable to do what you thought was best. *"Give, and it will be given to you. A good measure, pressed down, shaken together and running over, will be poured into your lap. For with the measure you use, it will be measured to you"* (Luke 6:38). This works in our relationship with God, and it works in a marriage relationship.

2. Own the decision. Finally you must make a decision. Once a decision is made, both of you must own that decision. Do not think that doing what they wanted removes your responsibility from the decision. Own it just as though it was your wish and your decision. You are responsible because you agreed.

3. Persuade, but do not force. Never force your mate to do anything. There is no place for force in a marriage. Each of you is an adult and has freedom of choice, no matter how bad it may seem at the time. If they want to leave, let them go. Do not stand in their way. If they want out of the car, as soon as you can get a safe place to stop, let them out. Persuade, but do not force.

What if you cannot decide, and you must decide, now? God placed the man in the leadership role and he must decide. Unless she is asked to violate her conscience, Godly women should submit. Do not think that this means the man gets his way if you cannot work out an agreement in time. It means he must decide. Godly men will often do what their wife wants.

Men, what if your wife does not submit? It depends on the situation. There are no easy answers to the question. However, this should send up a red flare there are problems in the dynamics of your marriage. One, you cannot reach agreement. And, two, you have no safety net when you cannot. This is a good time to sit down with another couple you respect and get some outside input. Learn to do it right and save yourself from future heartache.

Tough Issues

From the diagram at the right, it should be obvious which decisions will be the toughest to make. When the decision is extremely important to both of you and you cannot do both, what do you do? For example she wants both of you to go to her parents for the weekend, and he made plans with his parents for both of you for the same weekend. You cannot do both. You feel strongly that you should go together, and this is the last free weekend for several weeks. How can you make a decision that will leave both of you feeling good about the outcome?

He cares little She cares a lot	He cares a lot She cares a lot
Her decision	Tough choice
He cares little She cares little	He cares a lot She cares little
Doesn't matter	His decision

First, together, lay out the decision before God. Pray to God about the question and what you want. Laying our requests before God helps us to consider his input in the situation and solicits his help. Seek objective factors that might help you to decide this one. For example, Mom just got out of the hospital. Dad has all his family in town. Strive to make the decision that is best for your marriage, not just for you. If necessary, get advice from a couple that you both respect and trust. Get advice. But remember, the decision belongs to the two of you.

Four facts can help you in this situation, no matter how important the weekend is to both of you:

1. Both of you cannot have your way. One of you or both of you will be disappointed.
2. You will not die if you miss this weekend, though you and your parents may be disappointed.
3. There will be many other times similar to this one where a decision must be made.
4. Now you can strengthen your relationship. It is more important than the decision. If you cannot have your way, you sacrificed for a great cause.

Consider two observations:

One, life is not fair. Situations always differ, and anyone who spends a few seconds thinking can make a strong case detailing how unfairly they were treated. People with selfish tendencies, everyone, can argue persuasively that they got the raw end of the deal. Say no to your selfish voice, and make sure that your mate feels that they have been treated fairly.

Two, compensating the one that sacrifices helps them to feel your sense of fair play. Acknowledge their sacrifice. Resist the temptation to explain why their sacrifice is not that bad. Appreciate their sacrifice. Let them be disappointed. Do not make promises you cannot keep, but offer them a choice for the near future that may require sacrifice on your part.

Some Tips for Good Decision-Making Process:

1. Remember that your relationship is more important than this decision.
2. Follow the process without focusing on the outcome.

3. Think what is best for "us," not "me."
4. Be solution-oriented; find a way that will work.
5. Be persuadable.
6. Stay calm.
7. Use conversation voice; avoid inflammatory remarks.
8. Use constructive language.
9. Accept the final decision as your own.

Think about a recent important decision that you made together. Discuss how you think you did as a couple in each phase of the decision-making process. In general, how do you do with each phase?

a. Discovery phase

_____

_____

_____

b. Discussion phase

_____

_____

_____

c. Decision-making phase

_____

_____

_____

Additional thoughts, questions and insights...

6

Resolving Conflict

Goal: To learn to resolve the inevitable conflicts with my spouse in a way that heals our hurts and makes it easier to forget.

All Couples Experience Conflict

No two people getting married are exactly alike. Therefore, there will always be disagreements that must be worked out. The process of coming to agreement, called decision-making in the previous chapter, is not conflict. It may take more time than you would like, but it is not conflict. Try to make decisions and resolve disagreements without conflict.

Conflict, what many people would call a "bump," an argument or a fight, occurs in every marriage. How you handle it will significantly affect the quality of your relationship and your marriage. People fight about the strangest things. "You opened two boxes and we only needed one," he said. "Well, you didn't come home on time yesterday," she countered. "Yes and you never cook a nice meal anymore," he returned the jab. And this can go on and on. Senseless frustration, rage and malice pouring out of two people that have committed to love, honor and cherish each other.

What is going on? Why does it happen? How should I handle it? These are good questions. You can understand what is happening and why it happens. And you can learn what you should do when it happens.

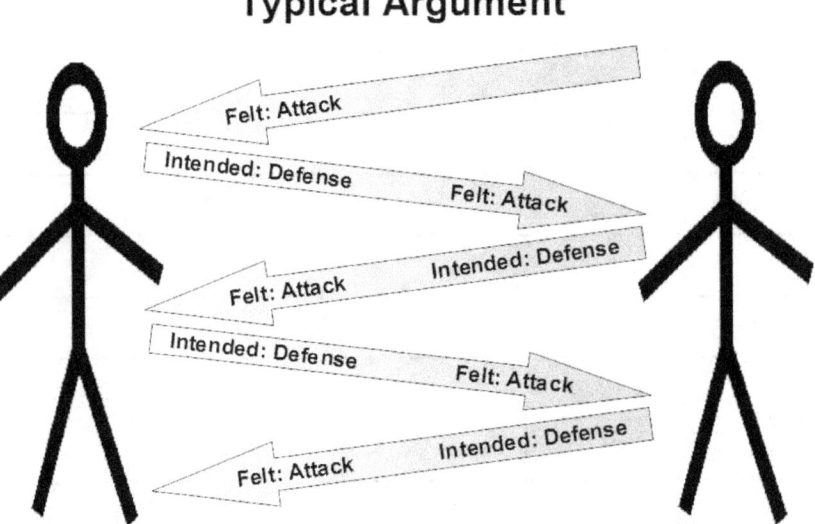

Typical Argument

Conflict generally feels like a series of attacks from which you must defend yourself. From the other person's point of view it is a mirror image. They see your defense as an attack. All the attacks and arguments connect in an endless stream of conflict. This takes the form expressed in the diagram at the right.

Everything is connected. "I did this because they did that. They did this because I did that." "She made me feel this." "He made me do that." All the attacks, wrongdoing, hurt feelings and responses hook together like a box of paper clips. The primary issue, the best intentions and a clear statement of what you want to do, all important facts, get lost in a tangled web of remarks. You get upset, frustrated and you get nowhere. When you try to resolve it, you pick up one paper clip and the entire box of paper clips comes with it. Resolving the conflict is nearly impossible.

Take a different view. Look at the conflict as a collection of injuries or hurts as pictured below (hurts can be far worse than what is implied by the Band-Aid representation). This view of a conflict helps you to see what is happening, the resulting damage and what must be resolved.

Yours	Theirs

Hurt What caused it? How did it hurt you?	Hurt What caused it? How did it hurt you?	Hurt What caused it? How did it hurt them?	Hurt What caused it? How did it hurt them?
Hurt What caused it? How did it hurt you?	Hurt What caused it? How did it hurt you?	Hurt What caused it? How did it hurt them?	Hurt What caused it? How did it hurt them?

Talk about each hurt and resolve it, one person at a time and one hurt at a time. When talking about a single hurt, do not connect it to another one. Understand the pain you caused and apologize for it, even if your intentions were not bad. Taking responsibility for causing hurt is a major step towards resolution. Explaining why you meant no harm, though sometimes helpful, can make your mate feel that you are unwilling to take responsibility for the harm you caused. This will not help resolve the issue and often causes further injury to your mate.

What Happens in a Conflict
1. **Injury** – Someone gets hurt. It can happen from a misunderstanding, an almost unpreventable situation, careless words, harsh words, a perceived tone or a variety of other ways.
2. **Pain** – Men as well as women suffer when they get injured. Emotional pain hurts as much, if not more, than physical pain. The pain produces very real suffering whether or not it is recognized or accepted by your mate.
3. **Anger** – Pain often leads to resentment and anger towards the person who caused the injury. Some people move quickly from the injury to anger without realizing the pain they feel; they just get mad. Anger, even when attempts are made to contain it, pours out of a person in the form of a raised voice, harsh tones or something similar
4. **Retaliation** – Though it may not be calculated, premeditated or purposely rooted in malice, anger often produces retaliation that strikes back with the aim to hurt. Because anger limits self-control and the ability to see events clearly, retaliation is usually stronger and more hurtful than intended. This four-step cycle repeats itself in your mate and, in a full-blown verbal fight, comes back at you with the speed of light.

Avoid Conflict...When You Can
The Bible compares reckless words to a sword (Proverbs 12:18). If your reckless words physically stuck your spouse with a sword, you would quickly find ways to stop. No one would stab their mate with a sword and then immediately ask to make love. No one would slash their mate and then scold them for not wanting to talk. However, far too many do this verbally. Even though the pain is emotional and often delayed, not physical and immediate, it is very real. Learn to recognize and understand "emotional injuries."

Stop It Where You Can!
Proverbs 12:18   *Reckless words pierce like a sword,*   *but the tongue of the wise brings healing.*

1. Do not injure! Newlyweds discover all kinds of ways that they unintentionally injure one another. Seek to avoid the things that hurt your spouse. The best way to resolve conflict is never to produce it.

For the one who caused the injury	For the one hurt by the injury
a. Ask yourself what you did that hurt them.	a. Why am I hurt?
b. Accept responsibility for what you made them feel.	b. Can I be less sensitive?
c. Do not blame what you did on something that they did.	c. Can I look at it from their perspective? (Why might I have done the same thing?)
d. Do not think, "Why did this hurt?"	d. Can I just "get over/forgive" the hurt?
	e. Did I misunderstand what they said?

2. Deal with the pain. God gives us physical and emotional pain for a reason. Figure out why and work it out.

For the one who caused the injury	For the one hurt by the injury
a. Do not expect immediate healing or quick fix.	a. Have I done something to hurt them?
b. Do not tell them why they should not be hurting or criticize them for hurting.	b. Figure out what it is that hurt you.
c. Treat emotional pain with as much concern as you would physical pain.	c. Express your hurt using speech that can be heard.
d. Their pain is not there to manipulate you.	d. Can I endure the pain without getting angry?

3. Anger management. Anger hurts you more than the person you are angry with.

For the one who caused the injury	For the one hurt by the injury
a. Look for the source of the anger, the hurt.	a. Do I need a time out?
b. Do not be self-righteous; remember when you have been angry.	b. Acknowledge to my spouse that I feel angry.
c. Do not expect it to disappear immediately.	c. Be angry and do not sin
d. Do a study in the Bible about anger.	d. Play by the rules

4. Damage control. Proverbs 29:11. Things said in anger cannot be unsaid. Verbal and physical abuse has no place in a marriage.

For the one who caused the injury	For the one hurt by the injury
a. Filter out the anger and seek the facts.	a. My anger is a verbal sword in my hand, do not use it.
b. Think about what you have done to contribute to this.	b. What would Jesus do?
c. Temper the messages since anger distorts the truth.	c. A fool gives full vent to his anger (Prov. 29:11)
	d. Think more, talk less.
	e. Express your feelings in constructive terms.

Learn to Filter Out the Anger

When your spouse is upset and speaking or reacting angrily, you can filter out the anger. Blocking out the anger and sifting through the personal put-downs for the facts will enable you to remain calm and to react helpfully. The temptation to return anger for anger and put-down for put-down certainly is compelling, but it can be resisted. Choose to be self-controlled. Considerable pain can be avoided. It is worth the effort to learn how you should listen to a frustrated and angry mate.

Use the following examples to help you develop this skill.

Screaming. *"I am sick and tired of cleaning up after you! I am not your mother. I do not appreciate being treated like a maid. You live like a slob. I cannot take this anymore. Why can't you pick up after yourself?"*

a. What are the implied messages in the comment you would do well to ignore?

_____

_____

b. What is she feeling?

_____

_____

c. What are the facts she is communicating to you?

_____

_____

Shouting. *"I cannot believe you spent $150 on your hair. Do you have any idea how many bills we have this month? Now we can never pay all of them. What were you thinking? Don't ever do that again!"*

a. What are the implied messages in the comment you would do well to ignore?

_____

_____

b. What is he feeling?

_____

_____

c. What are the facts he is communicating to you?

_____

_____

Apologies That Heal: More Than Saying You Are Sorry

Apologies help to heal the injuries and take away the pain. However, an apology requires more than saying, "I am sorry." Some people say, "I'm sorry," when they mean, "Move on," or "Get over it." A hollow apology is often followed by, "I *said* I was sorry." "What do you want from me?" And, "Why can't you forgive?" These attempts to apologize will not resolve conflict and, in fact, will likely hurt your mate.

Learn to apologize. This takes longer for some than for others, especially prideful people. Apologizing requires more humility than skill or finesse. At first, when you do it well, you may feel that you came away with more of the blame than you deserved. Though your spouse feels better, you may feel bad about yourself. Claiming your part of the blame makes you a person of integrity who loves the truth. Feel good that you have resolved your part of the conflict. Later, and it may take some help from others, you need to learn to resolve the inner conflict that you feel.

1. **Understand what you have done to hurt them.** Ask like an inquiring friend, not a lawyer on a cross-examination. Be patient and let them get it all out, even if they are expressing it in hurtful terms. Do not defend yourself. Help them by contributing what you did. "I blew it..., I was rude..., I put you down..., I embarrassed you..., I made you feel ugly..."
2. **Put it in your own words.** They know you understand when you tell them, in your own words, how you hurt them and why it hurt them. Do not minimize your wrongdoing. Do not make excuses, even valid ones. Focus on how you hurt them by what you said or did.
3. **Then tell them you are sorry.** Express sincerely that you are sorry for the specific thing you did. Continue to apologize until the hurt goes away. The better you get at apologizing, the less you will have to apologize. If you apologize seven times, and then complain that they have not forgiven you, you make it seem that your apology was not sincere. You imply that you are not really sorry, just eager for them to forget about your wrongdoing. Humble yourself and keep apologizing until the hurt is gone.

Express Your Hurts So They Can Be Heard

You make it much easier for your spouse when you express your hurt in non-inflammatory terms that do not injure. Learn to communicate your injury in a way that can be heard. Restate the thoughts below to make them easier to hear.

Why can't you ever remember anything I ask you to do? I can't believe you forgot to stop and buy bread on the way home. Now we have guests coming for dinner, and we have no bread. I can't trust you with anything. I knew I should have done it myself.

_____

_____

_____

Why did you tell me you were going to be home at 5:00 when you were going shopping? You never come home on time when you shop. I was counting on you to have dinner ready when you said. Now I am really late. You have ruined my whole evening. It is obvious that my plans mean nothing to you.

_____

_____

_____

Conflict produces hurt and pain that must be forgiven. God expects us to forgive each other. Getting hurt can be compared to getting a splinter in your foot. Getting it out may seem more painful than leaving it in there, but this is not true for the long term. Sometimes it is hard to tell if the splinter has been completely removed. Remember, it does not come out on its own. Learn to resolve your conflicts completely.

Signs that a conflict is resolved would include the following:
- Can talk about it in a normal tone
- Do not bring it up again
- Do not think about it

Set Your Limits

Matthew 12:37
*"For by your words you will be acquitted,
and by your words you will be condemned."*

Highways through mountainous terrain require guardrails to protect vehicles that lose control. In the same way, some self-imposed guidelines can save your marriage from serious injury if you follow them. Think through the guidelines that you would like to establish for your new family. Make sure you are willing to live by the rules you establish. Be realistic but carefully consider how you want to build. Once you finish your thoughts, discuss with your mate and decide together what you want. Get help for agreement if you need it.

The following exercise is designed to help you choose the standards you want to set for your relationship. Look at the following table. For each area, circle the box to the right that you believe most closely matches the standard you want to set for your marriage. The standards get higher as you go from left to right.

Area	1	2	3	4
Anger Management	No pushing, grabbing or physical force	No yelling or slamming things	Only brief outbursts or raised voice or harsh tone	No raised voice and no harsh tone
Shutting down	Can leave to collect yourself, always come back	Can walk away or leave, but must say when you will return	Can stop an argument but only if both of you agree	Can't stop talking during an argument
Statements that judge your mate	No venomous insults intended to hurt	Share only what you believe to be accurate	Constructive criticism only	Never say anything that could be perceived as a put-down

How will you handle the situation if your mate violates the standard you set together?

_____

_____

Learn to Build Each Other Up

Everyone possesses an emotional bank account. A smile, singing and generally feeling on top of the world accompanies an overflowing account. Doom, gloom, despair and depression indicate an overdrawn account. You make deposits and withdrawals on your mate's account whether or not you are aware of what you have done. Like a mirror reflects your image, in a very real sense, your mate reflects the balance of the daily transactions you have made to their account. While it is true that others affect your mate's account, your transactions are bigger since you are closer to them.

Everyone wants to live with a person whose account is overflowing. Some people would like to marry a person who is happy regardless of how little is in their account. These people react to an overdrawn account by telling their mate to "get happy," "fix it" or even "change your attitude." Oops, they just made another withdrawal.

Hurts make huge withdrawals. Criticisms make withdrawals that vary in size. Even small corrections make withdrawals. Neglect, simply the passing of time, decreases the balance.

Do you want to live with someone whose account is overflowing? Learn to make deposits. Realize that most deposits are very small. One withdrawal will require many deposits to cover the loss. So develop a lifestyle of making deposits, of building one another up.

In a marriage, the husband must encourage his wife and the wife must encourage her husband. Look at the following six ways you can build each other up.

1. **Do not make withdrawals.** Learn how to minimize the number of withdrawals you make. Find out what hurts them and stop doing it. Do not put them down or make fun of them, especially in front of others. Do not insult them. Building comes easier when you stop tearing down.

2. **Be sincerely grateful for them.** Make a list of fifty things you appreciate about your mate. Ponder and talk about those things. Pick one a day to share with them. Also share these in the presence of others. Some people consistently think about what they do not like about their

mate. They think it is acceptable to voice those complaints. This is not true. Even if you are critical only in your heart, much of the damage is already done. On the other hand, a grateful heart will consistently make deposits. When you live with someone, they will sense how you feel.

3. **Express affection to them.** Greetings and good-byes are very important. Use each one to express affection. A hug, a kiss and some words of affection should be your habit. Even during stressful times, expend the energy to give sincere affection. In this way, you will make many valuable deposits. However, never force a hug or a kiss. If they are not ready to hug or kiss, you have probably hurt them, and you will need to resolve it. Cards, flowers, letters and gifts also make substantial deposits. Remember special days.

4. **Let them know how much you need them.** Some people project such an independent spirit that they communicate to others that they do not need them. Rather, tell your mate how much you need them. To honor means to value, to hold in high esteem. Let them know how much you value specific things about them. Honor them. It is like money in the emotional bank.

5. **Believe in them.** A sincere, "You can do that!" can do wonders to build up your mate. Take an optimistic, subjective view of your mate. In this way you will endear yourself to them. Some, declaring themselves realists, may be thinking, "What if they cannot do that? Do you want me to lie?" You should never lie. However, you need to learn what it means to think subjectively. "She is the most beautiful woman in the world," does not require a beauty contest. Believing in your mate, taking an optimistic and subjective position about their ability builds them up.

6. **Give them the benefit of the doubt.** The US court system says "innocent until proven guilty." If people charged with a serious crime get the benefit of the doubt, surely you can do that for your mate. Assume the best. Do not assume they will make the same mistake again. Look for the best, and you will find it. Criticisms and doubts can become self-fulfilling prophecies. Build them up. Give them the benefit of the doubt!

Why is it important to build up your mate, to make deposits in their emotional bank account?

_____

_____

_____

What are the last three ways you have made deposits in your companion's account?

_____

_____

_____

How do you react when your emotional account is overdrawn?

_____

_____

_____

How does your companion react when their emotional account is overdrawn?

_____

_____

_____

Additional thoughts, questions and insights...

7

How Will You Spend Your Money?

Goal: To understand how my spouse and I deal with money and to find a mutually satisfying approach to our finances.

Ecclesiastes 5:10
*Whoever loves money never has money enough;
whoever loves wealth is never satisfied with his income.*

How you deal with money reveals a lot about your heart and your character. Selfish desires come clearly into view when couples seek to spend their money as one and not two. The love of money continues to produce "all kinds of evil." The struggle over how to spend your money will challenge your relationship. So learn God's view of money, and put it into your heart. Your ability to achieve financial unity in your marriage depends on it.

You have spent your whole life spending money and managing your finances. What is the big deal about marriage and finances? Well, what used to be one pool of money, one set of needs and wants, one set of preferences, one set of weaknesses and one set of values now becomes two. Now, another person has an interest in nearly every spending decision you make. What you considered insignificant, may be significant to your financial partner. The item you wanted might be exactly the one they could never live with. Simple decisions, especially during the first months of marriage, may require a lot of discussion. What is attractive to one may be hideous to another. That which is a "must have" to one may seem irresponsible to another. Your spending habits will change. Be flexible and eager to reach consensus, a place where both can feel good, or at least okay, about financial decisions.

What God Says About Money

1. **Remember that wealth comes from God (1 Chronicles 29:11–12).** This does not mean that one must be godly to acquire wealth. In fact, evil people were rich both in Bible times and today. It means that you should be grateful for what God gives you. It comes from God. The talents you have to make money came from God. Even the principles you may follow to succeed financially come from God. So use the money God gives you for his purpose.

2. **Watch out! Loving money is evil (Ecclesiastes 5:10; 1 Timothy 6:6–10, 17–19; 1 John 2:15).** God made people for you to love, not money or the things it can buy. The love of money brings "all kinds of evil." When you love money, you become a slave to that which you wish to own. Money can powerfully supply your needs, but it makes a horrible ruler for your life. When money rules your life, it destroys your character and your relationships. It causes wants to appear like needs, and it blinds you to the needs of others, especially your mate.

3. **Give cheerfully to God's work (1 Corinthians 9:11–14, 16:2; 2 Corinthians 9:7–8).** God wants us to be grateful for the privilege of giving to his work. God's church does wonderful things such as feeding the poor and putting lives back together. Your contribution provides one way for you to participate in this work. As God provides you with money, take his share from the top. Give generously and cheerfully to promote God's causes and God's work.

4. **Live within your means; be content in all circumstances (Philippians 4:11–19).** Do not spend more than you have. Your spending must be less than your income. This depends more on your convictions than it does on your level of income. Many people in this world have learned to live happily on a fraction of what you want to spend. Additional income will not solve your money problems. Learning to be content within your means will. Remember, he who loves money never has enough.

5. **God wants us to be generous with our money (2 Corinthians 9:11).** God tells us that generosity makes us rich. When we focus less on our needs and more on the needs of others, we can become generous. God wants couples to be generous, though couples must work to achieve consensus in their generosity. There are many awesome ways to be generous. Both people should be able to be cheerful about their giving so that the riches that come from giving can be enjoyed by both of you.

6. **Work hard (Acts 20:35; Proverbs 14:23, 21:5, 30:24–25).** God wants us to work hard so that we can meet our needs and help to meet the needs of others. He created us to do good works. Success in your job, in general, requires you to work hard. Managing your financial affairs well requires hard work. Talking decisions out until you reach agreement takes hard work, especially at first. Work smart, and work hard. Shortcuts are no substitute for hard work in God's view.

7. **Get lots of advice and count the cost before making large purchases (Proverbs 15:22; Proverbs 19:20).** Do your homework before you buy. Houses, cars, appliances and other big-ticket items require more research, thought and planning. Now that these decisions must be made for two, used by two and paid for by two, even more time will be required. Jesus uses a financial decision to illustrate how we must count the cost before making a decision to follow him. Do not expect all your advice to converge or agree. Good decisions are often a choice of many good options. Get the advice and create a plan to pay for the item you want to purchase. Any projections you make about your income in the future should be solid, a sure thing, not optimistic assumptions or hopes that may or may not happen. Good advice can help you to sort this out.

8. **Pay your debts (Romans 13:7–8).** The Bible speaks very clearly on this matter. Pay your bills on time. Never get yourselves into a situation where you are choosing between creditors, paying the nastiest first. Though unavoidable circumstances can cause this condition, most people arrive there because of a series of bad financial decisions that placed the value of what they wanted above a secure financial position.

9. **Provide for your family; save for your children (1 Timothy 5:8; 2 Corinthians 12:14).** Take care of your family. The Bible says that a person who does not take care of their family is worse than an unbeliever. Work hard and be ambitious to succeed but not to the detriment of your family. Do not neglect your family in the name of providing for them. And save "for your children." Put together a budget that includes saving. Put the money into an account that is not easily accessible. Work towards saving ten percent or more. Invest your savings wisely.

10. **Do to others as you would have them do to you (Luke 6:31).** An unselfish attitude provides a foundation for financial unity. Put the needs of your mate above your own (Philippians 2:3).

Do not be surprised when the two of you disagree on how to spend your money. Also do not be surprised at the time and energy it takes to reach agreement. Coming to consensus is essential for the unity of your marriage. Finances are a troublesome area for many couples. Do not take shortcuts. Though some of these may seem attractive and logical because they produce short-term gain, avoid them. Build your marriage on solid ground. Carefully consider each of these pitfalls. Do any of these describe your approach to finances or a temptation you face?

Financial Pitfalls

1. **Your money and my money** – Some people who get married keep separate bank accounts and continue to speak about your money and my money. This leads one to say, "It's my money, so I'll spend it the way I like." That was true when you were single. Your goal in marriage should be to make all that both of you own "ours." Combining the money into one account, though it may take longer to make some decisions at first, helps you to bond financially and make the transition from two to one. The decision to spend must rest with two and not just one.

2. **Selfishness** – Each of us has a strong desire to have what we want when we want it and to spend money the way we want to spend it. Financial unity cannot be achieved unless we control these selfish desires. Naturally, you can see clearly what you like and what you think is important. Selfishness blinds you to the financial desires of your mate. Only with work, and more work, can you see and understand the wants, needs and values of your mate. Even then, you can never completely understand their point of view. Develop an environment that allows you to talk calmly about the subject. Much dialog is required for you to begin to understand each other's values and wants. Do not be discouraged if it takes time for you to accomplish this.

3. **Secret spending** – The principle, "buy now and ask forgiveness later," will harm your marriage. While the principle will get you what you want now, it does many harmful things to your mate. It communicates that "I come first." Secondly, it conveys that you did not feel you could justify the purchase to your mate, but decided to buy it anyway. Thirdly, it tells your mate that you do not trust their judgment. Lastly, from a practical point of view, it changes the rules to: If you really want something, just go buy it. That philosophy will kill any budget.

4. **Worry about money** – Some people fret and worry about how the bills will be paid. One should be concerned about paying the bills and should figure out how to pay the bills. However, this should be a task, not a lingering, cannot-sleep, first-waking-thought kind of burden. Do not worry (Matthew 6:25). If you cannot figure out how to pay your bills, get help. Swallow the bitter pills that you must in order to get your finances under control.

5. **Continual desire for more** – Advertising unashamedly promotes greed. "You deserve one of these." "You are worth it." "No one should have to live without this." "Be the envy of your neighbors." 1 John 2:15 tells us not to love the world or the things in the world. A desire for more will pressure your finances no matter how much you make. Learning to be content with what you can afford removes the pressure on finances.

6. **Insistence on a pauper's lifestyle** – Some want to live miserly either out of conscience or simply because they do not like to spend money. Marriage changes the equation. Financial sacrifice must be a joint venture—both of you must agree. Do not expect your new partner to sacrifice the same way you do. It may be necessary for the two of you to make some additional financial sacrifices to meet your budget. Even then, make them in agreement. Do not expect your partner to be just like you, spending when you would spend and sacrificing in the areas where you would sacrifice.

7. **My decision because I make more** – Discussion about "who makes more" divides couples and wastes time. Further, it plants the ungodly idea that your value is tied to how much you make. The two become one regardless of the amount of anyone's salary.

8. **Spend more than you make** – The easy spending that credit cards provide may seem to be a "safety net" when financial difficulties arise. In reality, the safety net is a debt trap that can handicap your financial future. The high interest rate of credit cards makes them an unwise choice for financing debt. Pay them off every month or get rid of them. Do not spend more than you make. Watch out for impulse buying, recreational shopping and budget amnesia.

9. **Differing financial styles** – Life offers many ways to administer your finances, and there are numerous ways to spend your money. Not all decisions are a matter of right and wrong; they are personal choice. Some prefer to invest heavily in day-to-day items, others in special occasions, still others in hobbies or investments. One person's style differs from another. Learn to mold your styles into one. This means that both of you will have to change. Both of you will feel that as a couple you are overspending in some areas and underspending in others.

10. **Different financial goals** – Some people want to help as many people as possible. Others want to retire early so they can devote full time to another interest. Some people are content to live on a shoestring budget, just getting by. Others get very uncomfortable when savings fall below a safe cushion. You will likely start with differing goals. Learn what your goals are, and seek to identify your new goals as a couple. Work to find goals that both of you can live with.

About You: Finances

God wants to prosper you. How has he prospered you in your life?

_____
_____
_____

All wealth comes from God. How does this understanding affect your pursuit of more money?

_____
_____
_____

The Bible says that "the love of money is a root of all kinds of evil." How does it tempt you?

_____
_____
_____

Describe how you decide how much to give to God's work.

_____
_____
_____

How do you feel about that amount?

_____
_____

What are your goals in this area?

_____
_____
_____

How much debt do you have? Debt 1 _____ Debt 2 _____ Debt 3 _____ Debt 4 _____ Debt 5 _____

Total Debt _____

How did you acquire these debts?

_____

_____

_____

Are you a generous person? _____ Why do you say that?

_____

_____

_____

Would your mate consider you a hardworking person? _____ Would your friends consider you a hardworking person? _____ Why do they feel that way?

_____

_____

_____

What was your last large purchase? _____ Describe how you made the decision to purchase (i.e., how did you decide you needed it, how did you decide which one to purchase, how did you arrange to pay for it?).

_____

_____

_____

Have you ever been late on a payment? _____ How often does it happen? _____ Why does it happen?

_____

_____

_____

Do you make enough money to supply your needs? _____ Would your partner agree? _____ Why do they feel that way?

_____

_____

In five years, how much money do you think you will make? _____ What is your plan to achieve this?

_____

_____

_____

Do you have savings or investments? _____ How much? $_____ How is it invested? Provide details.

_____

_____

_____

How much cash do you generally carry with you? $_____
How much cash do you spend a week? $_____

How would you describe yourself? Tight, conservative, balanced, generous, extravagant. _____ Why?

_____

_____

_____

How would you describe your partner relative to the preceding question? _____ Why?

_____

_____

_____

Do you have a budget? _____ Describe how well you stick to it.

_____

_____

What are your financial goals? In five years? In twenty years?

_____

_____

_____

Your Net Worth?

	What You Own	Worth	Owed on it	(Worth) - (Owed)
1	House			
2	Car			
3	Furniture			
4	Property			
5	Whole life insurance policy			
6	Stocks and Bonds			
7	Savings			
8	Misc:			
9				
10				
11				
12	Debts: School loans			
13	Credit card balance payment			
14	Personal loan			
	Total			

Your Budget

Use the following table to detail your budget alongside the budget of your spouse-to-be. Then add the two, and put this in the third column to see how they combine. Use this information to create a budget for the two of you as a family.

	Budget Item	His	Hers	His + Hers	Going Forward
1	Salary				
2	Other income: Source				
3	Add rows 1 – 2 **Total income**				
4	Contribution				
5	Debts: School loans				
6	Credit card balance payment				
7	Loan payments				
8	Savings/investments				
9	Housing: House payment/Rent				
10	Oil/Gas				
11	Gas				
12	Electricity				
13	Water				
14	Phone				
15	Cell phone				
16	Furniture allowance				
17	Repair allowance				
18	Food				
19	Health insurance				
20	Life insurance				
21	House/Renter's insurance				
22	Car: Car Payment				
23	Insurance				
25	Gasoline				
26	Repair allowance				
27	Clothes allowance				
28	Cash allowance				
29	Gifts				
30	Health club				
31	Dates/Entertainment				
32	Retreats				
33	Gifts to charity				
34	Vacations allowance				
35	Miscellaneous				
36	Add rows 4 – 35 **Total Expenses**				
37	Row 3 minus Row 36 **+save /-excess**				

Additional thoughts, questions and insights...

8

A Man and a Woman

Goal: To understand the differences between men and women and my role in the marriage.

By now you have noticed that men and women differ in many ways. We look at situations differently, we feel things differently; and our bodies differ in appearance and makeup. These differences thrill us at times and frustrate us at others. God designed us to be a complementary pair.

Describe the Differences

In the following areas describe how you view the tendencies you would expect from women and men. How are they different? How are they similar?

Area	Women	Men
Dealing with feelings		
Conversation		
Self-esteem		
Watching television		
Sports		
Romance		
Friends		
Clothes		
Anniversaries		

    It is clear that men and women are different. Every person is different and every couple is different. Each couple must learn to form a team. As a member of the team, it is important to know your role. As times have changed, so have the typical roles expected from men and women. While there are no set rules for determining your role in the marriage, it is important that the two of you agree on the division of labor. Just as when you were single, the work must get done, even though you carry a full workload outside the home. Will he do it or will she do it? Is this fair? Am I carrying my share of the load? Fill out the following table, talk about it, agree on equitable shares and follow through. Men and women feel loved when their mate carries a fair share of the work. Failing to carry your share tends to make your mate feel used and disrespected.

Who Will Do What Chores

Fill out the following table with the percent of the time that you expect to do that chore compared with your spouse-to-be. For example, if you plan to do the grocery shopping three out of four times, put 75 in the % column. Add the other chores that are relevant to you.

Chores	%	Chores	%
House		**Social planning**	
Grocery shopping		Planning trips/vacations	
Putting groceries away		Buying gifts for family and friends	
Cooking meals		Inviting others over	
Cleaning up after meals		Planning weekend dates	
Emptying the dishwasher			
Vacuuming		**Finances**	
Cleaning the bathrooms		Paying the bills	
Washing clothes		Balancing the checkbook	
Ironing clothes		Filing and record keeping	
Putting clean clothes away		Taking care of the income tax	
Making the bed		Earning the family income	
Returning recyclables		Managing family investments	
Taking garbage outside			
Taking garbage to the curb		**Car**	
Cutting the grass		Car maintenance	
Planting flowers		Car insurance	
Shoveling snow		Car registrations	
Raking leaves		Car shopping	
Mopping/sweeping floors		Car financing	
Cleaning the basement			
Cleaning the garage		**Miscellaneous**	
Decorating indoors		Shopping for her clothes	
Painting the house indoors		Shopping for his clothes	
Painting the house outdoors		Buying computer equipment	
Buying furniture		Computer maintenance	
Buying a home/renting an apartment		Setting the alarm	
Securing home loans		Turning down the heat at night	

As the designer who completely understands both sexes, God created guidelines for our roles as husband and wife. While the chore lists today for men and women may be more similar than they were forty years ago, God's recipe for success has not changed. Though society may attempt to create unisex roles for today's couples, God's word continues to clearly specify different instructions for men and women.

Ephesians 5:22–23

Wives, submit to your husbands as to the Lord. For the husband is the head of the wife as Christ is the head of the church, his body, of which he is the Savior.

Society generally attacks God's plan in two ways. The first is to define the roles in an extreme manner, the husband as a slave-driving dictator using his wife to satisfy his every whim and the wife as a doormat with no rights or feelings who utters, "Yes, Master," to his every command. By defining the roles this way, they can be shown to be archaic, unreasonable and undesirable. Therefore, God's plan for marriage should be discarded because it no longer applies. God never intended this perversion of his plan.

The second way that society attacks God's plan is to water down the meaning of the roles until they have no real application. This approach may define the husband as the leader, but it limits his leadership to basically when the wife agrees with him. And it may define the wife's role as being submissive, but only when the husband is loving and effective in his leadership. This definition appeals to those who seek the appearance of putting the Bible into practice, but who lack the conviction to do what the Bible says when it differs from what appeals to their thinking on the subject.

What Does It Mean to Lead and to Submit

We have all been under the authority of another adult. In settings outside marriage, we know what we want from the person in authority over us. No one ever wants to serve under a slave-driving dictator. We want a person who takes responsibility and knows where he/she wants to go and makes it easy for us to follow. We want someone who values our input and our contribution. We want a leader who listens to us and considers our needs and concerns, but makes decisions for the good of the whole. We want one who puts the good of the whole above their own wants and needs.

Many of us have led at one time or another and know what we want from those we lead. We want people who are flexible, cooperative and helpful. We want those who willingly say what they are thinking, but who accept a "no" answer without pulling back or seeking ways to retaliate. We want to lead those who are respectful and make it easy to lead. We want team players who keep us informed. We do not want to lead someone who insists on competing with us or who constantly challenges our authority.

On the other hand, we do not want blind followers who do everything we say without thinking or discussing the downside they anticipate. We do not want to lead others who have no initiative and who sit and wait for the next set of instructions. We do not want to lead those who outwardly do what is asked, but inwardly harbor resentment and malice.

What does it mean to submit? What does it not mean? How has this been demonstrated in your relationship?

_____
_____
_____
_____
_____
_____
_____
_____
_____

What does it mean to lead? How has this been demonstrated in your relationship?

_____
_____
_____
_____
_____
_____
_____
_____
_____

Additional thoughts, questions and insights...

9

The Two Will Become One

Goal: To prepare to have a sex life that provides great satisfaction to my spouse and to me.

God's plan is amazing! From the very beginning, his plan included "the two becoming one flesh." Look at the following passage from Genesis, the first book in the Bible:

Genesis 2:24
For this reason a man will leave his father and mother
and be united to his wife, and they will become one flesh.

As you get ready to commit yourselves to each other in marriage, be confident that God has incredible plans for your sexual relationship and has provided the instructions to ensure success.

About You

Please answer a few questions that provide some information about you.

What do you include in your definition of sex?

_____
_____
_____

How do you feel about sex?

_____
_____
_____

Where did you obtain your knowledge about sex? (i.e., parents, school, TV, friends, book, etc.)
Have you read a book on sex? (i.e., *The Act of Marriage* by Timothy LaHaye)

_____
_____
_____

Please share any fears or concerns you have about sex in your upcoming marriage.

_____

_____

_____

_____

_____

What are the significant events in your life that have influenced how you feel about sex?

_____

_____

_____

_____

Do you have any habits or practices that might affect your sex life?

_____

_____

Do you have any health issues that will affect your sex life?

_____

_____

_____

What method of birth control have you chosen? Have you discussed this with your spouse-to-be?

_____

A Pornographic Society

Our society now speaks openly about sex. Conversations about sex, sexual innuendo and implicit sex scenes frequently confront Americans, beginning at an early age. All of this discussion of sex has become a strong influence in the lives of every person preparing to get married. The "adult films and magazines" view of sex, though still perverted and harmful, now streams from our primetime TV programs and PG films in movie theaters. Do not let these perverse myths that get presented as "well known" facts steal the joy from your sexual relationship. Find a mature godly couple you trust (mentoring couple), and ask all your questions. The truth will help you to wisely build the important sexual side of your relationship. No matter how much you think you know, if you really get frank, you may be surprised at what you can learn. Couples who give unselfishly to each other find the long-term satisfaction so many others talk about but cannot find.

What outstanding questions do you have about sex?

_____

_____

_____

_____

A Gift from God

One of the great blessings from God in marriage is the sexual relationship. God compares sex in marriage to a fountain or a cistern in Proverbs 5 where a person could come and drink to their fill. God's plan for marriage, when followed, produces real and continuing satisfaction, not just for one night, a few weeks or until kids arrive. Even in today's world of failed relationships and marriages that end in divorce, by following God's plan you can build a marriage that lasts and that satisfies each other sexually for a lifetime.

Proverbs 5:18–19
May your fountain be blessed,
and may you rejoice in the wife of your youth.
A loving doe, a graceful deer—
may her breasts satisfy you always,
may you ever be captivated by her love.

Sex possesses a wonderful magical quality; it bonds couples physically and emotionally. This quality misleads couples who engage in sex before marriage by convincing them that their relationship is stronger and deeper than it really is. But for married couples who develop a regular and satisfying sex life, this quality binds them together in a unique way that strengthens their relationship.

Sex can never provide a solid foundation for your relationship. God's plan builds on commitment, first to God, and then to each other, and creates an environment where your friendship can deepen for a lifetime. Commitment and friendship provide the perfect atmosphere for sex that satisfies and flourishes. Commitment says, "I love you, and I will be with you for the rest of my life. My staying with you does not depend on your beauty, your performance in bed or how perfectly you meet my needs. I commit myself to pleasing you."

The Differences Between Men and Women

God designed us to be complementary, perfect partners for sex. Certainly men and women differ widely in almost every aspect of sex, from our plumbing to our perceptions. While this makes sex exciting and wonderful, it frustrates couples who have not learned to understand their mate's needs. All people enter marriage knowing that there are significant differences between men and women, but few appreciate the depth of the differences until they have experienced years of marriage. Consider the following list of items as they relate to sex, and describe how you view the tendencies you would expect from women and men. How are they different? How are they similar?

Area	Women	Men
Recent conflict		
Visual stimulation		
Environment (lighting, mood, music)		
Foreplay		
Length in time of a sexual encounter		
Romance		
Connection of feeling loved and having sex		
Spontaneous sex		

Set the Table

Those who want to enjoy sex together must first learn to "set the table." When you get ready to have a great meal, you must first set the table in preparation. How you treat one another before you have sex is very important. Warm greetings, help with a dreaded chore, an affectionate kiss or some other expression of love prepares everyone, especially women, to be intimate. How women feel about themselves affects the way they feel about making love to their husbands. Many men have no idea how much is involved in building a great sex life together. A recently married man in New England wrote the following words.

"Prior to being married, I though the concept of a sexual relationship was a far simpler process for couples who are married. I was ignorant of the emotional component in the process and not aware of the differing perspectives between men and women. Shortly after being married I discovered the whole process of engaging in sex to be far more complicated. Being male with no experience in the matter, I guess I equated it with wanting to have a sandwich with someone and doing precisely that. Sure, there is choice of bread and other ingredients that may be unique to each individual. However,

having a sandwich is not dictated much by schedule, outstanding things to be done, interaction with others throughout the day, or feelings that stems from visiting one's memory about some non-related issues. I suspect that much of my perspective on the matter may be the result of what I derived from conversations and more importantly the movies, standard material (rated R, PG) and pornography since I had no other reference.

My ignorance of the emotional component surprised me the most. I discovered that arguments act as a short circuit to both of us (it probably impacts me the most). I do not readily enjoy the process of being close after an argument. Other emotional blocks stem from my wife's physical perspective of herself. This is a convoluted process because it can have its source in me, for example, not consistently complimenting her. Another has to do with my daily interaction with her. If she feels that I have not been sensitive to her or valued her feelings or other things like these, then our sexual relationship becomes a difficult process or no process at all.

Another observation I noted was the different perspective between men and women. Some of the purity problems, which I had prior to being married, still persist. I thought that a sexual relationship in marriage would obliterate that area of sin completely. I must admit that it has helped in some ways, but it has opened up new areas of struggles for me that I never before considered. I have learned that my wife, like most women, is completely in tune with the emotional nature of our relationship and derives as much from that as I do from sex. This I have yet to resolve in my mind, but I must conclude it is quite perplexing. This is exacerbated by the fact that the physical process does not lend itself to the degree of spontaneity that I had imagined because men and women are prepared for the process at differing times. This has served to challenge my selfishness. I had no idea that scheduling would have played such a significant role in the process for us but it has."

How can the husband set the table for a great marriage as well as a great sex life together?

_____

_____

_____

Communication About Sex

Giving feedback to your partner is very important. As individuals, we all have differing tastes. We feel things differently. We respond differently. And things change. Sometimes we may like one thing, and another day we may like something entirely different. This is very normal. It takes time to know what we like and what we want. This makes the job of pleasing your mate interesting and sometimes challenging. For this reason, your sexual life together can be enriched through the years as you grow in your ability to please each other. Again, this is normal and is what should happen.

How you provide feedback is very important.

Tell them what you like. Positive reinforcement not only makes your partner feel good, it guides them as to what pleases you. Everyone likes to hear, "I love it when you ____."

Use negative feedback sparingly, and try to combine it with a positive. "I like it much better when you ____." You can accomplish most of the same thing with positive feedback.

Do not use emotion in negative feedback. "Don't do that!" shouted at your mate can cause your mate to feel inept and want to stop making love altogether. "I do not like that. I would prefer this." These words, when spoken in love, can guide your mate without making them feel bad.

Exercise: Massage the shoulders of your mate. Allow them to tell you how they like it. After a couple of minutes, allow them to massage your shoulders as you guide them. Use this exercise as a precursor to understand how you can also communicate about the sexual relationship. (Because of the nature of this exercise, it might be best to do it in the presence of a mentoring couple.)

Your Body Is Not Your Own

Jesus asks us to deny ourselves and follow him. We learn from Paul in Philippians 2:3–4 that following Christ involves considering the needs of others and "in humility consider[ing] others better than yourselves." These instructions prepare Christians to be great lovers. Your role in lovemaking is to please your partner. This simplifies things. Rather than worrying about how well you are performing, focus on how to please your mate. Considerable satisfaction comes from simply pleasing your partner. Both are satisfied when they make love with this mindset.

1 Corinthians 7:3–4
The husband should fulfill his marital duty to his wife, and likewise the wife to her husband. The wife's body does not belong to her alone but also to her husband. In the same way, the husband's body does not belong to him alone but also to his wife.

Clearly, there must be give and take in successful lovemaking. God's plan involves two people giving to each other. You must allow and help your partner to please you. This means providing feedback in an encouraging way that helps them to successfully bring you pleasure. It means that you are concerned about them and their feelings, even when they are giving to you.

Intimacy

Sex involves a total giving of one's self in the most intimate way. However, having sex does not ensure intimacy. Couples must learn to be intimate by growing together, getting to know each other and by sharing openly what they think and feel inside.

What does it mean to be intimate?

_____

_____

_____

How does a couple's level of intimacy affect their sexual relationship?

_____

How does a couple's sexual relationship affect their level of intimacy?

How Often?

Couples routinely want to know how often to have sex. They want to know what is normal or average. The answer is that "normal" varies, not only from couple to couple, but also from time to time for a couple. The sexual appetite of a person naturally varies somewhat over time. It can also be affected by factors such as health and life (for example: emergency overtime at work). Each couple is different and must figure out what is right for them. Since no two people are alike, this process requires patience, understanding and sacrifice.

Honeymoons usually provide ample opportunity and a setting conducive to having sex. After this time couples eventually settle into what is normal for them. Often couples find that this varies from once to several times a week. Couples should be careful to avoid going for long periods of time without having sex. This exposes them to temptations such as lust and to insecurities, and it deprives them of God's blessings intended for married couples. Partners with stronger appetites than their spouse should be careful to avoid turning sex for their mate into a chore. Seek what is mutually beneficial.

Additional thoughts, questions and insights...

10

A Good Start

Goal: To establish good habits to help us build a great marriage.

Congratulations on completing this material! You know more about what to expect and have learned some tools and some ways of thinking that will help you deal effectively with the situations you will face in your marriage. The learning does not stop here. Each day will bring new growth opportunities that will challenge you and mature you as you continue to learn to live happily ever after.

Finally, develop some good habits that will serve you well. How you start your marriage is very important. A few good habits can take you a long way toward your goal of a happy marriage.

1. **Greet each other warmly when you leave and when you return.** This will set the tone for your interaction. It reassures your mate that you love them, respect them and are genuinely happy to see them. It affords ample opportunity for you to express affection, a key ingredient for successful marriages. Those who are not accustomed to this practice may find it tedious and may be doubtful of the benefit. Do it anyway. While you may not see the immediate effects from such a practice, time will make them clear.

2. **Make regular time to talk each day.** Find a regular time to talk. As simple as it sounds, many relationships could have been saved with this one activity. Talk about the day's decisions and who will do what. Over-communicate rather that assume. More importantly, take some time every day to share with each other what you feel and how you are doing. These personal discussions build intimacy and bind your hearts together. It is how we discover what is in our own heart as well as what is in the heart of our mate. It builds your relationship. No person remains the same. As one matures and changes, these discussions provide you with the opportunity to stay in lockstep with each other and to take your love for each other deeper, well beyond the love you share together today. Do not miss the obvious. Take some time every day to talk.

3. **Find ways every day to build each other up.** Sit down and make a list of the things you love about your mate. Do not stop at ten or twenty. Go for fifty or a hundred. It will amaze you to see just how much you love about your mate and how much you have to be thankful for. The process of writing these down helps you and directs your thinking. Then pick one item from the list each day, and find a creative way to express it to them. Do not patronize them or speak in general terms that have little meaning. Make your comments personal. Spend time every day thinking about how you can encourage your mate. Figure out what builds them up and do it. If you are not very good at this, keep trying. Practice will make you better. When two people spend their energy building each other up, life is really good. Do your part, and make it a daily habit to encourage your spouse.

4. **Go to bed and get up together.** There are obvious benefits from doing this and some that may not be so obvious. You build your sense of identity as a couple and create opportunities for conversation, snuggling and sex. You increase your discipline and you avoid the dangers of staying up late when all kinds of temptation abound. If one needs much more sleep than the other, at least do one together, preferably going to bed together. Though it may not always be possible, make it your practice, and you will be rewarded.

5. **Have sex regularly and often.** While this may seem like an odd thing to say, life gets busy, and selfishness can distract couples from this important gift from God. Stressful jobs, colds and flu, menstrual periods, children and many other issues can impact the perfect plan you bring into your marriage. Schedule times when you plan to make love. Though some may find the thought distasteful because they place a high priority on spontaneity, planning and scheduling will guard your time to be intimate. Planning and preparation play a key role in almost every phase of your life, and your sex life is no different. Careful planning and preparation can allow those special memorable moments to happen in a way that seems spontaneous. The sexual temptations will lose much of their allure when both of you feel satisfied. Do yourselves a favor, have sex regularly and often.

6. **Build your spiritual life together.** Marriage is the molding and the melding of two lives together into one. Though each person is responsible to God individually, marriage provides an opportunity for you to strengthen each other by sharing your spiritual lives together. Talking to God aloud together makes your spouse aware of your desire to please God, your fears, your dreams and how you feel toward God. When you do this daily, you grow together in your walk with God and with each other. You understand much more about the heart of your spouse, and you reveal much more about your own heart. Studying the Bible together on a regular basis can also strengthen your spiritual life. Two people have more insight into a passage than one does. Discussing what you read drives the message deeper into your heart and allows you to talk about your challenges and what the Bible says that addresses them.

    Sharing regularly in your prayers and your devotionals must be something that both of you want to do. It is not something that should be forced on an unwilling partner. Some find it challenging to share something so personal and feel hindered in their walk with God when they try to share it with their mate. Even so, it is worth the effort. Make it your goal to share in your most important relationship. Make sure that these times are used constructively. Do not use them for sessions to identify your mate's faults and what the Bible says to correct them. Use your mutual time to build each other up and to grow in your own knowledge and conviction. Few people will enjoy times that become fault-finding and fault-correcting missions. Feel free to share what you see in your life that you want to change, but do not make it your responsibility to point out what God says to them and what they should change.

Much more can be learned about how to have success in your relationship. Continue to learn, and each day will bring more knowledge your way. Sometimes the source will be the Bible or your spouse. Other times the source may be a book, a coworker, a friend, a situation, a problem, or even a child. Enjoy the love of your life, and be grateful for the gift God has given to you! Continue to learn and prepare to live as one!

Additional thoughts, questions and insights...

Also available at www.ipibooks.com

Also available at www.ipibooks.com

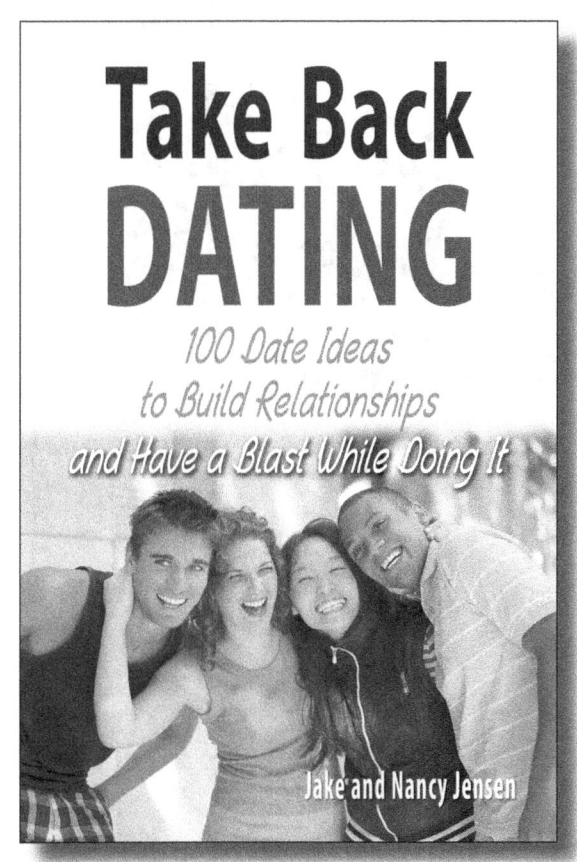

www.ipibooks.com
Orderline: (888) 932-4535

www.ingramcontent.com/pod-product-compliance
Lightning Source LLC
Chambersburg PA
CBHW081754100526
44592CB00015B/2433